D1492479

Guilt-Free
BAKING

To Nanny, who taught me to feed, to those close to me, who like to be fed, and to those who inherited the ability to put on weight just by looking at food!

First published in the United Kingdom and Ireland in 2015
by Nourish, an imprint of
Watkins Media Limited
19 Cecil Court
London, WC2N 4EZ

enquiries@nourishbooks.com

Copyright © Watkins Media Limited 2015
Text copyright © Gee Charman 2015
Photography copyright © Watkins Media Limited 2015

The right of Gee Charman to be identified as the Author
of this text has been asserted in accordance with the
Copyright, Designs and Patents Act of 1988.

All rights reserved. No part of this book may be reproduced
in any form or by any electronic or mechanical means,
including information storage and retrieval systems,
without permission in writing from the publisher, except
by a reviewer who may quote brief passages in a review.

Publisher: Grace Cheetham
Managing Editor: Rebecca Woods
Editor: Wendy Hobson
Art Direction & Design: Georgina Hewitt
Production: Uzma Taj
Commissioned photography: Matt Russell
Food Stylist: Gee Charman
Prop Stylist: Jo Harris

A CIP record for this book is available from the
British Library

ISBN: 978-1-84899-205-4

10 9 8 7 6 5 4 3 2 1

Typeset in Gotham
Colour reproduction by PDQ, UK
Printed in China

Notes on the Recipes
Unless otherwise stated:
Use medium eggs, fruit and vegetables
Use fresh ingredients, including herbs
Do not mix metric and imperial measurements
Recipes indicate the number of servings
Fat, saturated fat and calorie calculations are given
 for one serving
Spoons are level unless otherwise stated
1 tsp = 5ml   1 tbsp = 15ml   1 cup = 250ml

While every care has been taken in compiling the recipes for
this book, Watkins Media Limited, or any other persons who
have been involved in working on this publication, cannot
accept responsibility for any errors or omissions, inadvertent
or not, that may be found in the recipes or text, nor for any
problems that may arise as a result of preparing one of
these recipes. If you are pregnant or breastfeeding or have
any special dietary requirements or medical conditions, it is
advisable to consult a medical professional before following
any of the recipes contained in this book.

nourishbooks.com

Guilt-Free BAKING

Low-calorie and low-fat sweet treats

Gee Charman

NOURISH

EAT WELL, LIVE WELL

Contents

Introduction

As a chef, low-fat, low-calorie cookbooks were always the ones I walked straight past in the bookshop. It's not because I don't want to eat healthily – like everybody else, I have to watch what I eat. But after trying a few of them, it seemed that all the fun bits had been taken out. The food tasted like cardboard and had the texture of sawdust, and that seemed especially true of so many low-calorie and low-fat baking books.

I have inherited my mother's sweet tooth and I also just love to bake, so the option of having only one sweet treat a week – as many books suggest – is just never going to work for me, even though I am a firm believer in the 90 per cent good, 10 per cent bad rule when it comes to eating. So when I was approached about writing a book, this seemed like the perfect one to start with. It means I can bake to my heart's content without risking an expanding waistline.

I have to admit, however, that it has been a huge challenge. I didn't want to do what many books do and simply substitute butter for margarine, make the portions the perfect size for a mouse or cut out all the sugar and fill the recipes with artificial sweeteners. You can do that without my help with any cake recipe in any book. But it changes the texture beyond all recognition, the results lack flavour and the cakes are full of chemicals.

Instead, I started to think about reducing the amount of butter without cutting it out altogether, and looked for other sources of moisture for the cakes. Fruit purées have been a revelation, as they add natural sweetness and moisture to sponge cakes. However, in a plain vanilla sponge, a lot of the flavour comes from the butter, so big, punchy flavour-boosters are also needed. Spices like star anise and cinnamon and herbs like lemon thyme and basil fill the flavour void often created when you go low fat.

In traditional recipes, all sponges have the same texture, but one of the bonuses in this book is that adding low-fat yogurt, grated apple or puréed pears means the texture of each cake is different.

Some are light and fluffy, others are rich and sticky – but they are all delicious.

My grandmother loved to bake for other people and I think I have inherited that from her. While testing the recipes in the book, I often had five cakes on the go at once, so friends, family, neighbours and even my yoga class were often recipients of cake boxes full of sweet treats, which were gratefully received and scoffed by even the most avid of yogis!

Only on one occasion did my dad say, 'this tastes low fat'. But when I looked, he was eating a plain slab of sponge that was meant to be filled with yogurt and fresh fruit. After a little bit of structural engineering, where bites had been taken out of it, I managed to stack it up with all the 'fluffy bits', as he would say. Dad tucked in and I was back on track ... 'Oh yes, this taste good! And if this is low fat, I can eat more of it – right?' Well, no, Dad, but it's great that you are loving the cakes that much. I guess the moral of this story is that sometimes the individual elements of low-fat cakes may not work on their own, but adorned with the 'fluffy bits', they look and taste great.

With a growing obesity problem in the developed world, cutting down on the fat and calories we eat can't be a bad thing. What I am trying to do is keep all the good bits and just remove some of the bad. However, even low-fat, low-calorie cakes have to be eaten with a warning – just because the calories

are lower it doesn't mean you can eat ten! The benefit is that the treats you do have, you can have a little more often and they won't do you any harm, but they still have to be eaten as part of a healthy, balanced diet. I can't conjure up a way round that – sorry! But I have succeeded in using lots of oats, fruits and vegetables in these recipes, which is an added bonus in that they are both healthier and keep you fuller for longer. Plus they stop the sugar rush you get with traditional cakes, which are packed with sugar, making resisting a second helping a little easier.

Every recipe indicates the number of servings it makes, and each serving contains a maximum of 300 calories and 6g of fat – most a lot less. They also give you the preparation and cooking times – since most of these treats are served cold, that doesn't include the cooling time. If, like me, you find cakes are difficult to resist once they have cooled and are safely in the cake tin, I have tried to help by adding storage advice. Because some of us will be tempted to nibble too often at a cake that will remain at its best for a few days, many of the cakes can be made, a portion enjoyed, then the rest frozen for another day.

Whether it is for family and friends or for a sneaky treat on the sofa, baking should be a pleasure, and with my recipes it will be because it is all low in fat and low in calories – this is guilt-free baking at its best. So I wish you happy baking and – even more importantly – happy guilt-free eating.

gee x

Filling the Fridge & Freezer

Low-fat baking uses a lot of fruit, so my fridge is always filled with fresh berries. I also keep apples and pears in the fridge, but that's a personal choice as I like them cold and crunchy.

Although butter doesn't feature heavily in low-fat, low-calorie baking, I always keep a packet in the fridge. I also have a large pot of low-fat yogurt and lightest cream cheese, ready and waiting to make my cake batters and icings.

My freezer also is a treasure trove of goodies. Frozen berries are always in the freezer, as well as the fridge, ready for fruity bursts in cakes and bakes. I often make large batches of fruit purées and freeze them in ice cube trays before popping them out into a freezer bag. It means that I have them ready to hand and one stage of the baking process is already prepared. And when bananas get a little over-ripe, I peel and chop them, freeze them on a baking tray, then pop them in a freezer bag once they are frozen solid, so they are ready to make Instant Guilt-Free Banana Ice Cream (see page 21).

Once you have been through a baking spell, clear a space in your freezer as some recipes will quite happily sit in there for a few weeks or months, then at midnight when the sweet tooth craving hits, you don't need to reach for a chocolate bar but you will have homemade treats ready and waiting.

Because the cakes are just so tempting, it is sometimes a good idea to cool the cakes, then cut them into portions and wrap and freeze what you are not likely to use straight away – then you can't go for the 'it's a shame to leave just one slice' excuse. To help you, each recipe indicates how best to store the cake. They are all delicious freshly baked, of course, but if you do keep them, store the cakes in an airtight container, in the fridge if necessary, or wrap and keep them in the freezer.

Key to the symbols

 Best eaten fresh or within hours of assembling

 Store in an airtight container for up to the time indicated

 Store in an airtight container in the fridge for up to the time indicated

 Wrap and freeze for up to the time indicated

Stocking the Storecupboard

When it comes to baking, the storecupboard is your best friend. I have a designated cupboard in my kitchen that is bursting at the hinges.

The best thing about a packed storecupboard is that you can have all your dried ingredients ready to hand without needing to go out shopping every time you get the urge to bake. Plus, filling your cupboard with spices, dried fruits and nuts means that you can jazz up a plain sponge recipe at the drop of a hat.

One word of advice after years of baking is that I have learnt the value of plastic containers. Using them means that flour doesn't get everywhere as you try to close the bag and the open packet of nuts doesn't empty itself all over the kitchen floor as you go to grab it from the cupboard. Do label containers, though (I should have shares in marker pens) – otherwise you'll find yourself opening several boxes before you find the one you want or, as I have done, using plain flour when self-raising was required. Cakes don't look or taste quite the same if you make that mistake.

Here are a few storecupboard must-haves.

Flours & dry ingredients
- Baking powder
- Bicarbonate of soda
- Cocoa powder
- Cornflour
- Fast-action dried yeast
- Oats
- Plain flour
- Self-raising flour
- Strong bread flour
- Wholemeal flour

Fruit & nuts
- Desiccated coconut
- Dried fruits, such as apricots, cranberries, dates, raisins, sour cherries, sultanas, etc.
- Nuts, such as hazelnuts, pecans, salted peanuts and walnuts

Sweeteners
- Agave syrup
- Brown sugar, light and dark
- Caster sugar
- Clear honey
- Golden syrup
- Icing sugar

Spices & other ingredients
- Dark chocolate, 70% cocoa solids
- Light condensed milk
- Light evaporated milk
- Marshmallows
- Spices, such as cardamom, dried edible lavender, ground cinnamon, ground ginger, mixed spice, nutmeg, star anise
- Vanilla bean paste
- Vanilla extract (not essence or flavourings)
- White chocolate (just a little, mind you)

Basic Recipes

The guilt-free fundamentals

It is always good to have a few basic recipes up your sleeve. And the methods offered here can be easily incorporated into your own best-loved recipes to make them healthier – a favourite tart, for example, may be improved by a low-fat, low-calorie pastry.

All the recipes in this book are perfect to be served on their own but you might like to make up one of the basic recipes to complement the dish – French Apple Tart (see page 108) with Guilt-Free Vanilla Ice Cream (see page 20), for example, or Apple & Plum Crumble (see page 123) with Guilt-Free Vanilla Custard (see page 19).

But don't forget that basic doesn't mean boring – far from it. These are bedrock recipes that you will use over and over again.

Berry Coulis

PER SERVING:
  FAT 1G (OF WHICH SATURATES 0G)
  CALORIES 111KCAL
PREPARATION TIME: 10 MINUTES
COOKING TIME: 5 MINUTES

Put the berries, sugar, vanilla and 150ml/5fl oz/ scant ⅔ cup water in a saucepan over a low heat and warm through for a few minutes until the berries start to burst and release their juices.

Transfer the mixture to a blender and whizz until smooth, then rub the sauce through a sieve, using a wooden spoon or ladle to help you, and discard the seeds. Serve warm or leave to cool.

Makes about 300ml/10½fl oz/scant 1¼ cups
  (6 servings)

500g/1lb 2oz/4 cups berries, such as raspberries, strawberries, blueberries, blackberries or a mixture
100g/3½oz/scant ½ cup caster sugar
1 tsp vanilla extract

 7 days   3 months

Apple Purée

PER RECIPE QUANTITY:
FAT 1G (OF WHICH SATURATES 0G)
CALORIES 498KCAL (83 PER SERVING)
PREPARATION TIME: 10 MINUTES
COOKING TIME: 10 MINUTES

Put the apples, sugar and 100m/3½fl oz/scant ½ cup water in a saucepan over a medium heat and bring to the boil. Turn the heat down to low, cover with a lid and simmer for about 8 minutes until soft, adding a little more water if the apples become dry.

Drain off any excess water and mash with a fork to get a chunky purée or blend with a hand-held blender for a smooth purée. Leave to cool.

Makes 700g/1lb 9oz (6 servings)

6 eating apples, peeled, cored and cut
into 2cm/¾in dice
1 tbsp caster sugar
1 tsp ground cinnamon (optional)

 5 days 3 months

Pear Purée

PER RECIPE QUANTITY:
FAT 0G
CALORIES 330KCAL (55 PER SERVING)
PREPARATION TIME: 10 MINUTES
COOKING TIME: 10 MINUTES

Put the pears, sugar and 100ml/3½fl oz/scant ½ cup water in a saucepan over a medium heat and bring to the boil. Turn the heat down to low, cover with a lid and simmer for about 8 minutes until soft, adding a little more water if the pears become dry.

Drain off any excess water and mash with a fork to get a chunky purée or blend with a hand-held blender for a smooth purée. Leave to cool.

Makes 600g/1lb 5oz (6 servings)

6 eating pears, peeled, cored and cut
into 2cm/¾in dice
1 tbsp caster sugar

 5 days 3 months

Pavlova

PER SERVING:
FAT 0G
CALORIES 164KCAL
PREPARATION TIME: 15 MINUTES
COOKING TIME: 1½ HOURS, PLUS OVERNIGHT
COOLING IN THE OVEN

Preheat the oven to 110°C/225°F/Gas ½ and line a baking tray with baking paper. In a clean bowl, whisk the egg whites, using an electric mixer, until stiff peaks form. Gradually add the sugar and continue whisking until thick and glossy. Fold in the cornflour and vinegar.

Spoon the meringue onto the prepared baking tray and spread it out into a circle about 20cm/8in in diameter, creating a dip in the centre of the circle with the back of a spoon. Bake for 1½ hours, then turn the oven off and leave the pavlova to cool completely in the oven.

Makes a 20cm/8in pavlova (6 servings)

4 egg whites
225g/8oz/scant 1 cup caster sugar
1 tsp cornflour
1 tsp white wine vinegar

 14 days

Meringues

PER SERVING:
FAT 0G
CALORIES 59KCAL
PREPARATION TIME: 15 MINUTES
COOKING TIME: 1½ HOURS, PLUS OVERNIGHT
COOLING IN THE OVEN

Preheat the oven to 110°C/225°F/Gas ½ and line a baking tray with baking paper. In a clean bowl, whisk the egg whites, using an electric mixer, until stiff peaks form. Gradually add the sugar and continue whisking until thick and glossy.

Spoon the meringue onto the prepared baking tray in 12 neat piles. Bake for 1½ hours, then turn the oven off and leave the meringues to cool completely in the oven.

Makes 12 meringues (12 servings)

3 egg whites
165g/5¾oz/scant ¾ cup caster sugar

 14 days

Guilt-Free Shortcrust Pastry

PER SERVING:
FAT 2.5G (OF WHICH SATURATES 1.5G)
CALORIES 85KCAL
PREPARATION TIME: 15 MINUTES

Put the flour in a large bowl and rub in the butter, using your fingertips, until the mixture resembles coarse breadcrumbs. Stir in the sugar, then use a fork to mix in the ricotta and gently blend to a smooth dough, adding up to 1 tablespoon water, if necessary, a drop at a time, to bind the ingredients together. Wrap in cling film and chill for 10 minutes, or until required. Bake in a preheated oven at 180°C/350°F/Gas 4 or according to the recipe.

Makes enough for a 23cm/9in tart (12 servings)

200g/7oz/scant 1⅔ cups plain flour, plus extra for dusting
30g/1oz butter, chilled
1 tbsp caster sugar
4 tbsp ricotta cheese

 2 days

Guilt-Free Crème Pâtissière

PER SERVING:
FAT 1.3G (OF WHICH SATURATES 0.5G)
CALORIES 79KCAL
PREPARATION TIME: 5 MINUTES
COOKING TIME: 10 MINUTES

Warm the milk and vanilla extract in a saucepan over a low heat. Mix together the eggs, sugar and cornflour, then gradually whisk them into the warm milk. Pour the mixture into a clean saucepan over a low heat. Stir continuously until the mixture starts to thicken. It will go lumpy because of the cornflour, but stick with it and use a whisk and a bit of arm power to get rid of any lumps. Once it starts to bubble, cook for 30 seconds, then remove from the heat and spoon into a bowl. Cover the surface with cling film and leave to one side to cool.

Makes about 400ml/14fl oz/generous 1½ cups (6 servings)

350ml/12fl oz/scant 1½ cups skimmed milk
1 tsp vanilla extract
2 eggs
2 tbsp caster sugar
40g/1½oz/⅓ cup cornflour

 2-3 days

Guilt-Free Vanilla Custard

PER SERVING:
    FAT 2G (OF WHICH SATURATES 1G)
    CALORIES 90KCAL
PREPARATION TIME: 5 MINUTES
COOKING TIME: 10 MINUTES

Put the milk in a saucepan over a low heat. Scrape the seeds from the vanilla pod into the milk and add the vanilla pod. Mix together the cornflour, agave syrup and egg yolks, then gradually whisk them into the warm milk until blended. Remove the vanilla pod (when dry, you can put it in a container of sugar to make vanilla sugar).

Pour the mixture into a clean saucepan over a medium heat. Stir gently until the custard thickens, then remove from the heat immediately and pour into a jug. Do not leave it in the saucepan as the residual heat might cause it to curdle.

Makes about 500ml/17fl oz/2 cups (6 servings)

450ml/15½fl oz/scant 2 cups skimmed milk
1 vanilla pod, split in half lengthways
1 tbsp cornflour
3 tbsp agave syrup
3 egg yolks

 2–3 days

Guilt-Free Vanilla Ice Cream

PER SERVING:
    FAT 3G (OF WHICH SATURATES 1G)
    CALORIES 146KCAL
PREPARATION TIME: 10 MINUTES, PLUS AT LEAST
    6 HOURS FREEZING
COOKING TIME: 10 MINUTES

Put the milk in a saucepan over a low heat. Scrape the seeds from the vanilla pod into the milk and add the vanilla pod. Mix together the cornflour, agave syrup and egg yolks, then gradually whisk them into the warm milk until blended. Remove the vanilla pod. (When dry, you can put it in a container of sugar to make vanilla sugar.)

Pour the mixture into a clean saucepan over a medium heat. Stir gently until the custard thickens, then remove from the heat immediately and pour into a jug. Cover the surface with cling film and leave to cool to prevent it from forming a skin.

Pour the cooled custard into an ice cream machine and churn until frozen, then store in an airtight container in the freezer until needed. Alternatively, pour into a freezer container and freeze for 2 hours, then break up the ice crystals with a fork and freeze again for at least 4 hours.

Remove the ice cream from the freezer 15 minutes before serving to allow it to soften slightly.

Makes 650g/1lb 7oz (6 servings)

600ml/21fl oz/scant 2½ cups skimmed milk
100ml/3½fl oz/scant ½ cup light condensed milk
1 vanilla pod, split in half lengthways
3 tsp cornflour
3 tbsp agave syrup
3 egg yolks

 5 months

Instant Guilt-Free Banana Ice Cream

PER SERVING:
FAT 0.2G (OF WHICH SATURATES 0.1G)
CALORIES 120KCAL
PREPARATION TIME: 5 MINUTES, PLUS 4 HOURS
FREEZING
COOKING TIME: 10 MINUTES

Put the banana slices on a baking tray and pop into the freezer for 4 hours. Once frozen solid, put them in a blender with the agave syrup and start to blend. Pour the buttermilk through the funnel in the top of the blender and continue blending until smooth, then just serve – it's instant ice cream.

Makes 650g/1lb 7oz (6 servings)

5 bananas, cut into 1cm/½in slices
2 tbsp agave syrup or clear honey
100ml/3½fl oz/scant ½ cup buttermilk

Guilt-Free Frozen Vanilla Yogurt

PER SERVING:
FAT 1G (OF WHICH SATURATES 1G)
CALORIES 148KCAL
PREPARATION TIME: 10 MINUTES, PLUS 6 HOURS
FREEZING

Mix together the yogurt and condensed milk. Scrape the seeds from the vanilla pod into the mixture. (You can put the vanilla pod in a container of sugar to make vanilla sugar.) Pour into a freezer container, cover with a lid and freeze for 2 hours.

Remove from the freezer and mix with a fork to break down the ice crystals. Put it back in the freezer and leave for a further 4 hours, or until set.

Remove from the freezer about 15 minutes before serving to allow it to soften slightly.

Makes about 700g/1lb 9oz (12 servings)

500g/1lb 2oz/2 cups low-fat natural yogurt
200ml/7fl oz/scant 1 cup light condensed milk
1 vanilla pod, split in half lengthways

 5 months

Cupcakes, Muffins & Small Cakes

Good things come in small packages

I can't say I always agree with that statement, because when it comes to cakes it is often a case of the more the better, I say. But the beauty of cupcakes and muffins is that they are in their own perfect packages and there is no need to share, as everybody can have their own.

A few of the famous bakeries in New York have made cupcakes rather fashionable in recent years, when they had previously been seen as rather retro bakes that only the kids would make. Now they come in all shapes, sizes and colours and can look like little works of art.

Traditionally, cupcakes are covered in a thick layer of buttercream, but for those of us who only have to look at a cake for their top trouser button to pop open, buttercream is a no-go area. Instead, you have to get inventive and use lighter icing options, but that can be an advantage. If I'm honest, the cupcakes in the shop windows, with gravity-defying peaks of icing, are a little sickly even for my sweet tooth. So my options are all about a little more cake and a little less icing.

By baking your own, not only are you saving on the calories and grams of fat, guaranteeing all natural ingredients and enjoying far superior flavours, but you'll also find a saving in your pocket. When things are on trend, they become expensive so the money saved is an added bonus.

Victoria Sponge Cupcakes

PER SERVING:
FAT 4G (OF WHICH SATURATES 1G)
CALORIES 190KCAL
PREPARATION TIME: 30 MINUTES
COOKING TIME: 18 MINUTES

Simple, light and classic – these are so easy to make but unfailingly delicious.

Preheat the oven to 180°C/350°F/Gas 4 and line a muffin tin with paper cases or lightly spray the sections of a 12-hole loose-based mini sandwich tin with low-calorie cooking oil spray.

Mix together the flour and baking powder in a large bowl. Put the pears in a blender and blend to a purée. In a separate bowl, beat together the oil, caster sugar, eggs and vanilla extract, then add the pear purée and mix well. Add the wet ingredients to the dry ingredients and mix together well.

Spoon the mixture into the prepared muffin tin, filling the sections three-quarters full. Bake for 15–18 minutes until golden brown, well risen and a skewer inserted in the centre comes out clean. Transfer to a wire rack to cool.

Remove the paper cases, if necessary, and cut the cakes in half horizontally. If you like, reserve 6 strawberries for decoration, then hull and thinly slice the remainder. Spread a little of the jam over one half of each of the cut cakes, then top with a few strawberry slices. Replace the top of each cake and dust lightly with icing sugar. Cut the reserved strawberries, if using, in half, then make 3 cuts in each half up to the stalk but not going through it completely, then fan them out and put one on top of each cake to serve.

Makes 12 cupcakes (12 servings)

FOR THE SPONGE CUPCAKES:
low-calorie cooking oil spray, for greasing (optional)
250g/9oz/2 cups self-raising flour
2 tsp baking powder
150g/5½oz tinned pears in natural juice, drained
3 tbsp sunflower oil
150g/5½oz/⅔ cup caster sugar
2 eggs
2 tsp vanilla extract

FOR THE STRAWBERRY FILLING:
200g/7oz/1⅓ cups strawberries
6 tbsp low-sugar strawberry jam
1 tbsp icing sugar, sifted

 2 days 3 months without filling

Lavender Cupcakes

PER SERVING:
    FAT 4G (OF WHICH SATURATES 0G)
    CALORIES 160KCAL
PREPARATION TIME: 30 MINUTES
COOKING TIME: 18 MINUTES

Lavender gives a lovely subtle fragrance to these little cakes. You will find dried edible lavender in the baking aisle in major supermarkets or online.

Preheat the oven to 180°C/350°F/Gas 4 and line a 12-hole muffin tin with paper cases.

Mix together the flour, baking powder, salt and bicarbonate of soda in a large bowl. Grind the lavender to a fine powder in a pestle and mortar, then add to the flour mixture. In a separate bowl, whisk together the sugar, yogurt, vanilla bean paste, milk and oil. Add the wet ingredients to the dry ingredients and mix together well.

Spoon the mixture into the prepared muffin tin and bake for 15–18 minutes, or until a skewer inserted in the centre comes out clean. Transfer to a wire rack to cool.

To make the icing, mix together the icing sugar and food colouring, if using, then gradually work in enough of the lemon juice to make a thick but spreadable paste. Spoon the mixture onto the centre of each cake, then help it out to the edges using the back of a spoon. Decorate each cupcake with a sprig of lavender, if you like, then leave to set before serving.

Makes 12 cupcakes (12 servings)

FOR THE LAVENDER CUPCAKES:
200g/7oz/scant 1⅔ cups self-raising flour
1 tsp baking powder
½ tsp fine sea salt
½ tsp bicarbonate of soda
2 tsp dried edible lavender
100g/3½oz/scant ½ cup caster sugar
225g/8oz/scant 1 cup fat-free natural yogurt
2 tbsp vanilla bean paste
4 tbsp skimmed milk
3 tbsp sunflower oil

FOR THE LEMON & LAVENDER ICING:
100g/3½oz/heaped ¾ cup icing sugar, sifted
a drop of natural purple food colouring (optional)
2–3 tbsp lemon juice
12 tiny dried lavender sprigs on the
    stalks (optional)

 2 days 3 months without icing

Coffee Butterfly Cakes

PER SERVING:
FAT 4.5G (OF WHICH SATURATES 0.7G)
CALORIES 173KCAL
PREPARATION TIME: 30 MINUTES
COOKING TIME: 18 MINUTES

Makes 12 cupcakes (12 servings)

FOR THE COFFEE CAKES:
225g/8oz/heaped 1¾ cups self-raising flour
2 tsp baking powder
400g/14oz tinned pears in natural juice,
    drained
150g/5½oz/heaped ¾ cup light soft brown sugar
2 eggs
3 tbsp sunflower oil
2 tbsp very strong, cold black coffee
    or 1 tbsp coffee essence

FOR THE CREAM CHEESE TOPPING:
1 tbsp instant coffee or 2 tbsp coffee essence
100g/3½oz light cream cheese
1½ tbsp icing sugar, sifted

 1 day 3 months without icing

Butterfly cakes make a nice alternative to their more trendy cousins, the cupcakes. They look beautiful and use less icing than traditional cupcakes. For somebody who only started drinking coffee at the age of 28, it might seem odd that coffee cake has always been my firm favourite. A little bit of me was lost when my favourite store stopped making their coffee cake loaf when I was at school. In fact, that may be what forced me to become a chef and an enthusiastic baker. It is best to use a deep muffin tin and muffin cases for these so that you can use all the mixture and have plenty of cake for your butterfly wings.

Preheat the oven to 180°C/350°F/Gas 4 and line a 12-hole muffin tin with paper cases.

Mix together the flour and baking powder in a large bowl. Put the pears in a blender and blend to a purée. In a separate bowl, whisk together the brown sugar, eggs, pear purée, oil and coffee, using an electric mixer, until light and fluffy. Add the wet ingredients to the dry ingredients and mix together until just combined.

Spoon the mixture into the prepared muffin tin, filling the sections three-quarters full. Bake for 15–18 minutes until well risen, golden brown and a skewer inserted in the centre comes out clean. Transfer to a wire rack to cool.

To make the topping, dissolve the coffee, if using, in 1 tablespoon boiling water, then leave it to cool to room temperature. Beat together the cream cheese and 1 tablespoon of the icing sugar until soft, then beat in the coffee or coffee essence to taste until well blended. Cover and leave to chill in the fridge.

Using a small, sharp knife, press the point into the top of the cake at a slight angle, then cut round to remove a shallow upside-down cone from the top of each cake. Remove these in one piece, cut them in half, then leave to one side. Spoon or pipe the topping into the hole on top of each cake, then push the two halves of the cone into the icing at an angle so they look like butterfly wings. Lightly dust with icing sugar, if you like, to serve.

Chocolate Cupcakes with Avocado Frosting

PER SERVING:
FAT 4.5G (OF WHICH SATURATES 0.8G)
CALORIES 111KCAL
PREPARATION TIME: 30 MINUTES
COOKING TIME: 12 MINUTES

You are going to have to trust me on this one. I know avocado seems an odd substitute for a buttercream icing but it really works. It's smooth and creamy, and avocados naturally have such a delicate flavour, you quickly taste the chocolate over avocado. Of course, I know these are actually vegan cupcakes but I just didn't want to use that word as it would put so many non-vegans off the recipe immediately. For once, you won't miss butter and eggs in this recipe. The cakes are truly moreish and amazingly moist. Try them once and you'll see.

Preheat the oven to 180°C/350°F/Gas 4 and line two 12-hole mini-muffin tins with paper cases.

Mix together the almond milk and vinegar in a large bowl and stir well, then leave to one side for a few minutes to curdle. Beat in the sugar, oil, vanilla extract and almond extract, if using, and whisk until frothy. In a separate bowl, mix together the flour, cocoa powder, baking powder and bicarbonate of soda. Add the wet ingredients to the dry ingredients and mix together well.

Spoon the mixture into the prepared muffin tins, filling the sections three-quarters full. (Try spooning the mixture into a piping bag, cutting off the end, then piping it in.) Bake for 10–12 minutes until a skewer inserted in the centre comes out clean. Transfer to a wire rack to cool.

To make the frosting, scoop out the avocado flesh into a small blender or food processor (or bowl and work with a hand-held blender). Add the cocoa powder and honey and process until smooth, then gradually add a little almond milk, a drop at a time, until the mixture just begins to hold its shape.

Makes 24 mini cupcakes (12 servings)

FOR THE CHOCOLATE CAKES:
240ml/8fl oz/scant 1 cup almond milk,
    plus extra for the frosting
1 tsp cider vinegar
185g/6½oz/heaped ¾ cup granulated sugar
3 tbsp sunflower oil
1 tsp vanilla extract
½ tsp almond extract (optional)
250g/9oz/2 cups self-raising flour
30g/1oz/⅓ cup cocoa powder, sifted
1 tsp baking powder
1 tsp bicarbonate of soda

FOR THE AVOCADO FROSTING:
2 ripe avocados
4 tbsp cocoa powder, sifted
2 tbsp clear honey
a little almond milk, to loosen

 2 days ❄ 3 months without filling

Spoon the frosting into a piping bag fitted with a 1cm/½in star nozzle and pipe the frosting onto the centre of the cakes in a nice high peak. You do not need to cover the entire surface of the cake as this would add too much icing and therefore too many calories. Then peel back the paper and enjoy – the great thing is they are so mini you can eat two.

Apple & Star Anise Cupcakes

PER SERVING:
FAT 4G (OF WHICH SATURATES 1G)
CALORIES 157
PREPARATION TIME: 30 MINUTES, PLUS
AT LEAST 20 MINUTES INFUSING
COOKING TIME: 18 MINUTES

I think the range of spices available is under-used in baking. Don't get me wrong, I love traditional cakes, but if you want something a little different, adding spices is an easy way to create new flavours while keeping the fat and calories low. In this recipe, the star anise balances out the sweetness of the apples and is a great way of spicing up the unusual topping. I promise you, you won't even miss buttercream icing.

Put the milk and star anise in a small saucepan over a low heat and bring to a simmer. Remove from the heat, cover and leave to infuse for about 20 minutes, or better still overnight. Preheat the oven to 180°C/350°F/Gas 4 and line a 12-hole muffin tin with paper cases.

Beat together the eggs, sugar and vanilla extract in a large bowl, using an electric mixer, for about 5 minutes until light and creamy. Gradually pour in the oil, whisking continuously, then discard the star anise from the milk and whisk that in too. Use a large metal spoon to gently fold in the flour and baking powder, then stir in the apple cubes.

Spoon the mixture into the prepared muffin tin, filling the sections three-quarters full. Bake for 15 minutes until golden brown and firm to the touch. Leave to cool in the tin for 2 minutes, then transfer to a wire rack to cool completely.

Meanwhile, to make the topping, put the apples in a saucepan over a medium heat with 1 tablespoon water, the sugar and 1 star anise. Bring to the boil, then turn the heat down to low, cover with a lid and simmer gently for about 5 minutes until the cooking

Makes 12 cupcakes (12 servings)

FOR THE APPLE & STAR ANISE CAKES:
80ml/2½fl oz/⅓ cup skimmed milk
1 star anise
2 eggs
125g/4½oz/heaped ½ cup caster sugar
1 tsp vanilla extract
3 tbsp sunflower oil
150g/5½oz/1¼ cups plain flour
2 tsp baking powder
3 eating apples, peeled, cored and cut into
    1cm/½in cubes

FOR THE SWEET APPLE TOPPING:
1 cooking apple, such as a Bramley, peeled,
    cored and finely diced
2 eating apples, peeled, cored and finely diced
1 tbsp caster sugar
13 star anise (12 optional)
1 tsp cornflour or arrowroot

 2 days 3 months without topping

apple has broken down and created a purée, while the eating apple chunks stay whole. Mix the cornflour to a paste with 1 tablespoon water, then stir it into the pan and cook for a further 1 minute, stirring continuously. Remove from the heat and leave to cool. Spread the apple mixture on top of the cakes and serve with a star anise on each one, if you like.

Strawberries & Cream Cupcakes

PER SERVING:
FAT 3G (OF WHICH SATURATES 1G)
CALORIES 136KCAL
PREPARATION TIME: 30 MINUTES
COOKING TIME: 10 MINUTES, PLUS 2 HOURS
FOR THE STRAWBERRY CRISPS

Strawberries and cream are a match made in heaven – but cream is usually a no-go area in low-fat recipes. So here's a solution – use cream from a squirty can. It is aerated, so it looks great and saves you whisking, plus it is naturally lighter and you need less. The strawberry crisps look and taste amazing as they concentrate the natural flavour.

Preheat the oven to 100°C/200°F/Gas ½ and line a baking tray with baking paper. Spread the strawberry slices on the prepared tray and dust lightly with icing sugar. Bake for 2 hours until dark red and dry. Loosen from the paper while they are still pliable, then leave to cool and go crisp. Turn the oven up to 180°C/350°F/Gas 4 and line two 12-hole mini muffin tins with paper cases.

To make the cakes, put the strawberries in a blender and blend until smooth, then pass the purée through a sieve, using a ladle to help you, and discard the seeds. Mix together the flour and baking powder in a large bowl. In a separate bowl, whisk together the sugar, eggs, strawberry purée and oil, using an electric mixer, until light and fluffy. Add the wet ingredients to the dry ingredients and mix together until just combined.

Spoon the mixture into the prepared muffin tins and bake for 8–10 minutes until well risen and a skewer inserted in the centre comes out clean. Transfer to a wire rack to cool.

Just before serving, squirt a little aerosol cream onto the top of each cake and finish with some diced strawberries. Add a couple of strawberry crisps to each cake, if you like.

Makes 24 mini cupcakes (12 servings)

FOR THE STRAWBERRY CRISPS (OPTIONAL):
12 strawberries, hulled and finely sliced
2 tsp icing sugar, sifted

FOR THE STRAWBERRY CUPCAKES:
150g/5½oz/1 cup strawberries, hulled
175g/6oz/heaped 1⅓ cups self-raising flour
2 tsp baking powder
100g/3½oz/scant ½ cup caster sugar
2 eggs
3 tbsp sunflower oil

FOR THE STRAWBERRY CREAM TOPPING:
125ml/4fl oz/½ cup light aerosol real dairy cream
150g/5½oz/1 cup strawberries, hulled and finely diced

  3 months before assembling

Peach Melba Cupcakes

PER SERVING:
FAT 1G (OF WHICH SATURATES 0.7G)
CALORIES 148KCAL
PREPARATION TIME: 30 MINUTES
COOKING TIME: 15 MINUTES

These cupcakes are summer in a paper case. Full of sweet peaches and tangy raspberries, they are perfect for using up either the slightly hard or the over-ripe peaches in the bottom of the fruit bowl.

Preheat the oven to 180°C/350°F/Gas 4 and line a 12-hole muffin tin with paper cases or spray the sections of a 12-hole loose-based mini sandwich tin with low-calorie cooking oil spray.

Beat together the eggs, sugar, yogurt and vanilla extract in a large bowl, then fold in the flour, cinnamon and baking powder. Finely dice the peaches and stir them into the mixture.

Spoon the mixture into the prepared muffin tin, filling the sections three-quarters full. Bake for 12–15 minutes, or until a skewer inserted in the centre of the cakes come out clean. Transfer to a wire rack to cool.

To make the sauce, put the raspberries and icing sugar in a blender and blend to a purée, then pass the mixture through a sieve, using a ladle to help you, and discard the seeds. Remove the cakes from the paper cases. If you are serving them as a dessert with a fork, serve the sauce separately. Alternatively, spoon the sauce into a syringe (you can get one at your local chemist) or a piping bag with a really fine nozzle and from the side of the cakes, pipe some of the sauce into the centre. (If you do it from the bottom, it runs out and looks messy from the top.)

Makes 12 cupcakes (12 servings)

FOR THE PEACH CUPCAKES:
low-calorie cooking oil spray, for greasing (optional)
3 eggs
125g/4½oz/heaped ½ cup caster sugar
200g/7oz/heaped ¾ cup fat-free natural yogurt
1 tsp vanilla extract
225g/8oz/heaped 1¾ cups self-raising flour
1 tsp ground cinnamon
2 tsp baking powder
3 peaches, peeled and pitted

FOR THE RASPBERRY SAUCE:
200g/7oz/1⅔ cups raspberries
1 tbsp icing sugar, sifted

 2 days 3 months without the sauce

Black Forest Cupcakes

PER SERVING:
FAT 6G (OF WHICH SATURATES 2G)
CALORIES 212KCAL
PREPARATION TIME: 45 MINUTES
COOKING TIME: 15 MINUTES

Here's a modern recipe inspired by a blast from the past. Black Forest gâteau was the signature dessert of the late 70s and early 80s but it is now enjoying a revival – along with its companion, the prawn cocktail. (For those too young to remember, the main course was steak and chips!) With my version, even those watching the calories don't need to resist this delicious treat (especially if you use water instead of kirsch).

Preheat the oven to 180°C/350°F/Gas 4 and line a 12-hole muffin tin with paper cases. Put the pears in a blender and blend to a purée.

Mix together the flour, baking powder and cocoa powder in a large bowl. In a separate bowl, whisk together the sugar, eggs, pear purée and oil. Add the wet ingredients to the dry ingredients and mix until just combined.

Spoon the mixture into the prepared muffin tin, filling the sections three-quarters full. Bake for 12–15 minutes until risen and springy to the touch. Transfer to a wire rack to cool.

To make the filling, put the cherries and kirsch in a small saucepan over a low heat for a few minutes until starting to soften. Remove from the heat and leave to cool. Drain the cherries, reserving the liquid.

Use a small, pointed knife to cut out an upside-down cone from the top of each cake, around 2cm/¾in in diameter. Remove these in one piece. Fill the holes with some of the cooked cherries, then cut off and discard the points of the cone and replace the tops on the cakes. Drizzle over a little of the cherry cooking juices.

Makes 12 cupcakes (12 servings)

FOR THE CHOCOLATE CUPCAKES:
150g/5½oz tinned pears in natural juice, drained
150g/5½oz/1¼ cups self-raising flour
1 tsp baking powder
30g/1oz/⅓ cup cocoa powder, sifted
150g/5½oz/heaped ¾ cup light soft brown sugar
2 eggs
3 tbsp sunflower oil

FOR THE CHERRY FILLING:
200g/7oz/heaped 1¼ cups dark red cherries, pitted and finely chopped
2 tbsp kirsch or water

FOR THE CREAM CHEESE ICING:
100g/3½oz light cream cheese
1 tbsp icing sugar, sifted
½ vanilla pod, split in half lengthways
12 cherries
30g/1oz dark chocolate, 70% cocoa solids, grated

 2 days 3 months without filling or icing

To make the icing, mix together the cream cheese and icing sugar. Scrape the seeds from the vanilla pod into the mixture, then spoon it into a piping bag fitted with a 1.5cm/⅝in star nozzle. Pipe a small blob of icing just off centre on the top of each cake and top with a cherry and a sprinkling of grated chocolate.

Marshmallow Cupcakes with Meringue Frosting

PER SERVING:
   FAT 2G (OF WHICH SATURATES 0G)
   CALORIES 220KCAL
PREPARATION TIME: 45 MINUTES
COOKING TIME: 15 MINUTES

This is a great recipe if you want to avoid butter icing or if you just fancy a change. If you substitute the milk with almond, soy or rice milk, then the cakes become a vegan-friendly offering – don't say I don't think of you! Just check the labels to make sure that you are using totally vegetarian ingredients. You will need a sugar thermometer for making these cupcakes. The icing will develop a crust if you leave them for a day or so but they will still be soft and gooey in the centre.

Preheat the oven to 180°C/350°F/Gas 4 and line a 12-hole muffin tin with paper cases.

Whisk together the eggs, caster sugar, milk, oil and vanilla extract in a large bowl. Mash the bananas with a fork, then mix them into the egg mixture. Add the flour, cocoa powder, baking powder, bicarbonate of soda and salt, then add the marshmallows and fold all the ingredients together.

Spoon the mixture into the prepared muffin tin, filling the sections three-quarters full. Bake for 12–15 minutes, or until a skewer inserted in the centre comes out clean. Transfer the cakes to a wire rack to cool.

To make the icing, put the egg whites, lemon juice, granulated sugar and 2 tablespoons of warm water in a large, heatproof bowl set over a pan of gently simmering water, making sure the bottom of the bowl does not touch the water. Whisk, using an electric mixer, until the mixture reaches 70–75°C/158–167°F on a sugar thermometer. Once you reach that temperature, remove from the heat and either transfer to

Makes 12 cupcakes (12 servings)

FOR THE MARSHMALLOW CUPCAKES:
2 eggs
150g/5½oz/⅔ cup caster sugar
5 tbsp skimmed milk
1 tbsp sunflower oil
1 tbsp vanilla extract
2 very ripe bananas
225g/8oz/heaped 1¾ cups plain flour
2 tbsp cocoa powder, sifted
1 tbsp baking powder
1 tsp bicarbonate of soda
¼ tsp fine sea salt
30g/1oz mini marshmallows

FOR THE MERINGUE FROSTING:
3 egg whites
1 tsp lemon juice
150g/5½ oz/heaped ⅔ cup granulated sugar
a few drops of food colouring (optional)
30g/1oz white mini marshmallows

 2 days 3 months without frosting

a standard mixer or continue with an electric hand mixer to beat the eggs for 12–15 minutes until stiff, glossy peaks form. Whisk in a few drops of food colouring, if you like. Spoon the icing into a piping bag fitted with a large star nozzle and pipe onto the cupcakes. Scatter with the remaining mini marshmallows to serve.

Go Fruity Muffins

PER SERVING:
  FAT 5.6G (OF WHICH SATURATES 0.6G)
  CALORIES 172KCAL
PREPARATION TIME: 15 MINUTES, PLUS
  15 MINUTES SOAKING
COOKING TIME: 20 MINUTES

These are a perfect breakfast all-in-one treat – fruit, oats and apple juice in every mouthful. Remember not to overmix the batter when making muffins or they tend to go a little tough and rubbery. Keep it light in every way! The main difference between a cupcake and a muffin is that muffins are usually made with liquid fats, such as sunflower oil, and are not iced, whereas cupcakes are made with butter and are usually topped with mounds of butter icing. The fruit in these muffins can be changed to suit your own tastes and there is no need for icing.

Preheat the oven to 180°C/350°F/Gas 4 and line a 12-hole muffin tin with paper cases. Put the oats in a bowl, pour over the apple juice and leave to soak for 15 minutes.

In a separate bowl, mix together the flour, baking powder and bicarbonate of soda. In a third bowl, beat together the oil, sugar, eggs and vanilla extract, using an electric mixer, until light and creamy. Add the soaked oats and the egg mixture to the flour and mix together until just combined, taking care not to overmix as this will make your muffins tough. Gently fold in the fruit.

Spoon the mixture into the prepared muffin tin and sprinkle with the sunflower seeds. Bake for 20 minutes until risen, golden brown and just firm to the touch. Transfer to a wire rack to cool.

Makes 12 muffins (12 servings)

75g/2½oz/¾ cup rolled oats
150ml/5fl oz/scant ⅔ cup apple juice
185g/6½oz/1½ cups self-raising flour
1 tsp baking powder
1 tsp bicarbonate of soda
3 tbsp canola or sunflower oil
75g/2½oz/⅓ cup golden caster sugar
2 eggs
1 tsp vanilla extract
100g/3½oz/scant ¾ cup raspberries
100g/3½oz/⅔ cup blueberries
1 eating apple, peeled, cored and finely diced
1 tbsp sunflower seeds

 4 days

Clementine & Cranberry Muffins

PER SERVING:
FAT 5G (OF WHICH SATURATES 3G)
CALORIES 171 KCAL
PREPARATION TIME: 15 MINUTES
COOKING TIME: 20 MINUTES

With all that clementine zest and juice, your kitchen will smell like Christmas when these muffins are baking. If clementines are not in season, just use one large orange instead so that you can enjoy these treats all year round.

Preheat the oven to 180°C/350°F/Gas 4 and either line a 12-hole, deep muffin tin with paper cases or baking parchment, or place 12 non-stick mini loaf cases on a baking tray.

Mix together the flour, baking powder and sugar in a large bowl. In a separate bowl, mix together the cranberries, clementine zest and juice, melted butter, eggs and yogurt. Stir the wet ingredients into the dry ingredients until just combined, taking care that you do not overmix as this will make your muffins tough.

Spoon the mixture into the prepared muffin tin and bake for 15–20 minutes, or until a skewer inserted in the centre comes out clean. Transfer to a wire rack to cool, then dust with a tiny sprinkling of icing sugar to serve.

Makes 12 large muffins (12 servings)

250g/9oz/2 cups self-raising flour
2 tsp baking powder
100g/3½oz/scant ½ cup caster sugar
50g/1¾oz/scant ½ cup dried cranberries
grated zest and juice of 4 clementines
50g/1¾oz butter, melted
2 eggs
200g/7oz/heaped ¾ cup low-fat natural yogurt
a little icing sugar, sifted, for dusting

 4 days

Banana Bread Flower Pots

PER SERVING:
FAT 1G (OF WHICH SATURATES 0G)
CALORIES 300KCAL
PREPARATION TIME: 20 MINUTES, PLUS 3 HOURS
    RISING
COOKING TIME: 25 MINUTES

You are probably looking at this recipe and thinking, 'I'm never going to make these – it's far too much trouble to go all the way to the garden centre and spend £10 on flowerpots!' Well, if you are, you are a person after my own heart. I am a chef, but my heart does sink when I see a random piece of equipment or an ingredient that demands a separate journey to gather your wares before you can start messing up the kitchen and cooking. But I made this recipe for a big breakfast for a good friend's birthday, and the good old internet came up trumps, with mini flowerpots delivered to my door the next day. But if yours is not a special occasion, you can easily shape the dough into rolls and pack them together on a baking tray, or use a muffin tin – not quite as cute but just as tasty.

Put the bananas and vanilla extract in a blender with 3 tablespoons of the honey and blend to a smooth purée. Tip into a measuring jug (unless your blender is calibrated) and top up with warm water so that you have 350ml/12fl oz/scant 1½ cups liquid.

Mix together the flour, yeast, salt and sugar in a large bowl, then make a well in the centre. Pour in the puréed bananas and start to mix together until you have a soft but not sticky dough. Turn the dough out onto a lightly floured work surface and knead for about 10 minutes, or until the dough is smooth and elastic. Lightly oil a large bowl with low-calorie cooking oil spray. Put the dough in the bowl, cover with cling film and leave to rise in a warm place for 2 hours, or until doubled in size.

While the dough is rising, grease the insides of the flowerpots with low-calorie cooking oil spray. Do this two of three times to really 'season' the pots

Makes 12 buns (12 servings)

3 large ripe bananas
2 tsp vanilla extract
120g/4¼oz clear honey
500g/1lb 2oz/4 cups strong white flour,
    plus extra for dusting
7g/¼oz/2 tsp fast-action dried yeast
1 tsp fine sea salt
2 tsp light soft brown sugar
low-calorie cooking oil spray, for greasing
12 mini terracotta flowerpots, 5.5cm/2¼in diameter
    (new and unused in the garden, obviously)

 2 days

well. Cut out small discs of baking paper and put them in the bottom of each one to make it easier to remove the bread once it is cooked.

Turn the dough out onto a lightly floured work surface, knock the air out by punching it with your fist, then divide it into 12 equal pieces and roll into fat sausage shapes. Put each sausage into a flower pot, bunch the pots closely together in a baking tray, then cover lightly with baking paper. Leave to rise for a further 1 hour, or until doubled in size once again and nicely filling the pots.

Preheat the oven to 180°C/350°F/Gas 4. Bake for 25 minutes until golden brown and hollow-sounding when you tap the tops. Turn the bread out and drizzle over the remaining honey. Serve warm as an amazing breakfast bread.

Iced Buns

PER SERVING:
FAT 3.25G (OF WHICH SATURATES 1G)
CALORIES 299KCAL
PREPARATION TIME: 20 MINUTES, PLUS 3 HOURS
RISING
COOKING TIME: 15 MINUTES

Food – and especially baked goods – have always been a currency and a bargaining tool in our family. When my bottom was small enough to fit in the seat of a shopping trolley, an iced bun was my reward for behaving well at the supermarket. After Mum had done her shopping, I would be wheeled over, in my food-filled chariot, to the bakery counter to choose which one I wanted ... which was always the biggest one!

Mix together the flour and salt in a large bowl, then rub in the butter, using your fingertips, until the mixture resembles fine breadcrumbs. Stir in the sugar and yeast. Make a well in the centre of the flour and add the beaten egg followed by the milk and gently blend to a soft dough.

Turn the dough out onto a lightly floured work surface and knead for 10 minutes until the dough is smooth and elastic. Lightly spray a clean bowl with a little low-calorie cooking oil spray. Put the dough in the bowl, cover with cling film and leave to rise in a warm place for 2 hours, or until doubled in size.

Line a baking tray with baking paper. Turn the dough out again, knock the air out of the dough by punching it with your fist, then divide it into 12 equal-sized pieces. Shape them into sausage shapes and put them on the prepared baking tray, just touching. Cover the buns lightly with a piece of baking paper and leave to rise in a warm place for a further 40 minutes to 1 hour, or until doubled in size.

Preheat the oven to 200°C/400°F/Gas 6. Remove the baking paper cover and bake the buns for

Makes 12 buns (12 servings)

FOR THE BUNS:
500g/1lb 2oz/4 cups strong white flour,
    plus extra for dusting
1 tsp fine sea salt
35g/1¼oz butter
80g/2¾oz/⅓ cup caster sugar
7g/¼oz/2 tsp fast-action dried yeast
1 egg, beaten
200ml/7fl oz/scant 1 cup skimmed milk
low-calorie cooking oil spray, for greasing

FOR THE ICING:
225g/8oz/heaped 1¾ cups icing sugar, sifted
a few drops of natural food colouring (optional)
3 tbsp sugar strands

 2 days 3 months without icing

10–15 minutes until golden brown and risen and hollow-sounding when tapped on the base. Transfer to a wire rack to cool.

When the buns are cool, make the glaze. Put the icing sugar in a small bowl and gradually add 2 tablespoons water, a drop at a time, to make a stiff but spreadable paste. Add a few drops of natural food colouring, instead of some of the water, if you like. Dip the tops of the buns in the icing, then put on a piece of baking paper or a plate, dipped-side up. Sprinkle with sugar strands and leave to set before tucking in.

St Clement's Drizzle Cakes

PER SERVING:
FAT 4G (OF WHICH SATURATES 0.3G)
CALORIES 155KCAL
PREPARATION TIME: 15 MINUTES
COOKING TIME: 20 MINUTES

Lemon drizzle cakes are fresh and tangy, and are perfect if you want a cake that will last for a few days after baking. The sticky syrup that you pour over the cooked cake adds moisture, which is also helped by the courgettes in the batter. This is a twist on a plain lemon drizzle cake, with extra sweetness added by the orange zest and juice.

Preheat the oven to 180°C/350°F/Gas 4 and line 12 mini loaf tins with baking paper or mini loaf tin liners.

Whisk together the sugar, eggs and oil in a large bowl for 3 minutes, using an electric mixer, until light and creamy, incorporating as much air as possible. Gently fold in the flour, bicarbonate of soda and the lemon and orange zest and mix well, then stir in the courgette.

Spoon the mixture into the prepared loaf tins and bake in the centre of the oven for 15–20 minutes until well risen and just firm to the touch, or until a skewer inserted in the centre comes out clean. Cover with a clean tea towel and leave to cool in the tins for 5 minutes, then transfer to a wire rack.

Meanwhile, to make the topping, put the lemon and orange juice and agave syrup in a small saucepan over a low heat and bring to the boil, then simmer gently for a few minutes until the liquid is reduced by half and becomes slightly sticky. Slowly spoon the syrup over the warm cakes so that it soaks into the sponge. Serve warm or at room temperature.

Makes 12 cakes (12 servings)

FOR THE LEMON & ORANGE CAKES:
150g/5½oz/⅔ cup caster sugar
2 eggs
3 tbsp sunflower oil
200g/7oz/scant 1⅔ cups self-raising flour
1 tsp bicarbonate of soda
grated zest of 2 lemons
grated zest of 1 orange
1 courgette, grated, about 150g/5½oz total weight

FOR THE LEMON & ORANGE SYRUP:
4 tbsp lemon juice
juice of 1 orange
2 tbsp agave syrup

 3 days 3 months

Pumpkin Puffs with Salted Pumpkin Seeds

PER SERVING:
FAT 5.5G (OF WHICH SATURATES 0.8G)
CALORIES 173KCAL
PREPARATION TIME: 30 MINUTES
COOKING TIME: 45 MINUTES

This cake was born of a mistake when writing another recipe for this book. I had run out of paper cases so thought I would cook the mixture in piles on a baking tray just to see if the balance of spices was right. Like all good cooking mistakes – tarte tatin being my favourite example – a new recipe was formed and here it stands, a perfect breakfast treat to enjoy with a morning cup of tea.

Preheat the oven to 180°C/350°F/Gas 4 and line a baking tray with baking paper.

Toss the diced pumpkin with the cinnamon, mixed spice and 1 tablespoon of the oil. Tip out into an ovenproof dish and roast for 30 minutes until tender. Transfer to a food processor and blend until smooth. Cover and leave to cool to lukewarm.

Put the pumpkin seeds in a dry saucepan over a low heat for a few minutes just until they start to turn glossy, then sprinkle with the salt, toss together, then turn out onto a plate, crushing the mixture between your fingers.

Mix together the flour and baking powder in a large bowl. In a separate bowl, whisk together the sugar, syrup, egg, the remaining oil and the cooled pumpkin purée. Add the wet ingredients to the dry ingredients and mix together well.

Put 12 spoonfuls of the mixture onto the prepared baking tray, leaving a 5cm/2in gap between each one. Sprinkle over a few of the toasted pumpkin seeds and bake for 15 minutes until puffed and springy to the touch. Transfer to a wire rack to cool slightly, then serve warm or at room temperature.

Makes 12 puffs (12 servings)

250g/9oz peeled and deseeded pumpkin
or butternut squash, diced
1 tsp ground cinnamon
1 tsp mixed spice
4 tbsp canola or sunflower oil
2 tbsp pumpkin seeds
1 tsp fine sea salt
260g/9¼oz/heaped 2 cups self-raising flour
1½ tsp baking powder
85g/3oz/scant ½ cup light soft brown sugar
2 tbsp golden syrup
1 egg

 2 days 3 months

Biscuits & Cookies

Ready, steady, dunk!

That was the traditional school game at lunch and tea-time. We used to sit with our biscuit of choice and chosen hot drink, set the timer and get dunking. It was a bit like Russian roulette, as we wanted to hold on long enough to win but not so long that our biscuit broke off and sunk, wasted, to the bottom of the mug. I like to think that we were just taking science and maths out of the classroom as, after years of practice, we decided that it all came down to biscuit density, weight and angles – well that was my excuse for devouring a whole packet in one go.

The big problem with biscuits is that they are so easy to eat with every cup of tea from about 11am to 5pm. Because they are often small and unfilling, they easily disappear without us even thinking about the calories we are swallowing, so for my biscuits, I decided the fewer the calories in each one the better.

Each recipe in this chapter makes 24 biscuits but because, as I said, I can never stop with one, I have made all the servings two biscuits each, but each serving still falls below the 300 calories and 6g of fat limit. So what are you waiting for? Get dunking.

Iced Lemon & Lavender Biscuits

PER SERVING:
   FAT 3.3G (OF WHICH SATURATES 2.1G)
   CALORIES 130KCAL
PREPARATION TIME: 20 MINUTES, PLUS
   20 MINUTES CHILLING
COOKING TIME: 15 MINUTES

As a kid I used to make iced lemon biscuits at the weekend when friends came over – it was Mum's way of keeping us all quiet. These are based on the recipe I used all those years ago but with the sophisticated twist of the lavender.

Put the butter, syrup and lemon juice in a saucepan over a low heat until the butter has melted. Mix together the flour, baking powder, cream of tartar, granulated sugar, lavender and lemon zest in a bowl. Pour the melted butter mixture over the dry ingredients and mix to a smooth dough, adding a drop of skimmed milk, if necessary. Roll the dough into a ball, flatten slightly, wrap in cling film and chill in the fridge for up to 20 minutes.

Preheat the oven to 180°C/350°F/Gas 4 and line a large baking tray with baking paper.

Turn the dough out onto a lightly floured work surface and roll out to 1cm/½in thick. Use a 5cm/2in round pastry cutter to cut out 24 biscuits, re-rolling any off-cuts. Put the biscuits on the prepared baking tray and bake for 12 minutes until they start to turn golden brown and begin to become firm to the touch. Leave to cool on the tray for 5 minutes, then transfer to a wire rack to cool completely.

Meanwhile, put the icing sugar in a small bowl and the lemon juice in a separate bowl. Gradually mix the juice into the icing sugar, a drop at a time, to create a paste slightly thicker than double cream so that it can stick to the biscuits. Add a little food colouring, if you like. Drizzle the icing in lines across the biscuits and sprinkle with chopped lavender. Leave to set for 10 minutes before serving.

Makes 24 biscuits (12 servings)

FOR THE LEMON & LAVENDER BISCUITS:
50g/1¾oz butter
2 tbsp golden syrup
2 tbsp lemon juice
175g/6oz/heaped 1⅓ cups plain flour,
   plus extra for dusting
½ tsp baking powder
½ tsp cream of tartar
60g/2¼oz/¼ cup granulated sugar
1 tsp dried edible lavender
grated zest of 1 lemon
a drop of skimmed milk (optional)

FOR THE LEMON ICING:
50g/1¾oz/heaped ⅓ cup icing sugar, sifted
2 tsp lemon juice
a few drops of lilac food colouring (optional)
a few lavender sprigs, chopped (optional)

 3 days

Lime Fingers

PER SERVING:
  FAT 3.3G (OF WHICH SATURATES 2.1G)
  CALORIES 130KCAL
PREPARATION TIME: 20 MINUTES, PLUS
  20 MINUTES CHILLING
COOKING TIME: 15 MINUTES

We tend to use lemon in baking a lot while limes seem to be reserved for G&Ts – perhaps because the taste of limes can turn a little bitter when cooked, instead of giving that refreshing sharp flavour of the lemon. That's why lime is always added to curries at the end of cooking. However, these little limey fingers are cooked for such a short time that the lime becomes fragrant rather than bitter and the tangy icing gives the whole thing an extra boost and a limey kick.

Put the butter, honey and lime juice in a small saucepan over a low heat until the butter has melted. Mix together the flour, baking powder, cream of tartar, granulated sugar and lime zest in a bowl. Pour the melted butter mixture over the dry ingredients and mix together to make a smooth dough. Roll the dough into a ball and flatten it down. Wrap in cling film, then chill in the fridge for up to 20 minutes.

Preheat the oven to 180°C/350°F/Gas 4 and line a baking tray with baking paper.

Turn the dough out onto a lightly floured surface and roll out to 1cm/½in thick. Cut into 24 finger shapes about 2 x 5cm/¾ x 2in, re-rolling any off-cuts. Put the biscuits on the prepared baking tray and bake for 12 minutes until they start to turn golden brown and begin to become firm to the touch. Leave to cool on the tray for 5 minutes, then carefully transfer to a wire rack to cool completely.

Meanwhile, make the icing. Put the icing sugar in a small bowl. Gently squeeze 1–2 teaspoons lime juice into a separate bowl, then gradually mix it into

Makes 24 biscuits (12 servings)

FOR THE LIME BISCUITS:
50g/1¾oz butter
2 tbsp clear honey
2 tbsp lime juice
175g/6oz/heaped 1⅓ cups plain flour,
  plus extra for dusting
½ tsp baking powder
½ tsp cream of tartar
60g/2¼oz/¼ cup granulated sugar
grated zest of 1 lime

FOR THE LIME ICING:
50g/1¾oz/heaped ⅓ cup icing sugar, sifted
1 lime

 7 days

the icing sugar, a drop at a time, to create a paste just slightly thicker than double cream so that it can stick to the biscuits. Dip one end of each biscuit into the icing, then lay the biscuits on a wire rack. Finally, use a fine grater to grate the lime zest over the icing, then leave to set.

Jaffa Cakes

PER SERVING:
FAT 6G (OF WHICH SATURATES 2G)
CALORIES 141KCAL
PREPARATION TIME: 1 HOUR, PLUS 20 MINUTES
WHISKING AND 2 HOURS CHILLING
COOKING TIME: 18 MINUTES

'Full moon, half moon, total eclipse' – one of my favourite adverts that instantly bring Jaffa cakes to mind. In the old days, when my hips did not expand at the mere sight of an extra calorie, I could devour a whole packet of Jaffa cakes, taking my time to nibble around the edge, pick off the chocolate with my teeth, eat the jelly then the sponge – disgusting, I know, but it delayed having to tidy my room.

Line a 30 x 20cm/12 x 8in Swiss roll tin with cling film. To make the jelly, put the orange juice and agave syrup in a saucepan over a low heat and bring to a simmer. Simmer for 5 minutes, or until reduced by one-third. Soak the gelatine in cold water for a few minutes until soft. Squeeze out the excess water, then add the sheets to the pan and stir until dissolved. Pour into the prepared tin, cover with cling film and chill in the fridge for 2 hours until firm.

Preheat the oven to 180°C/350°F/Gas 4 and line a 35 x 25cm/14 x 10in cake tin with baking paper.

Put the sugar and eggs in a heatproof bowl set over a saucepan of gently simmering water. Beat for 15–20 minutes, using an electric mixer, until light and fluffy and doubled in size. You should be able to drip a W shape from the whisks that should remain on the surface for 8 seconds.

Put the butter in a saucepan over a low heat until it starts to bubble, then slowly drip it into the egg mixture, whisking all the time. Fold in the flour, taking care not to overmix. Spoon the mixture into the prepared tin, swirling the tray to spread it out thinly and evenly. Bake for 8–10 minutes until golden brown and springy. Transfer to a wire rack to cool.

Makes 24 cakes (12 servings)

FOR THE ORANGE JELLY:
250ml/9fl oz/1 cup smooth orange juice
2 tbsp agave syrup or caster sugar
2 sheets of gelatine

FOR THE SPONGE:
75g/2½oz/⅓ cup golden caster sugar
3 eggs
30g/1oz butter
125g/4½oz/1 cup plain flour

FOR THE TOPPING:
75g/2½oz dark chocolate, 70% cocoa solids
a little low-calorie cooking oil spray, for greasing

 3 days

Use a 6cm/2½in round pastry cutter to cut out 24 discs of the sponge and put them on a wire rack set over a sheet of baking paper. Wipe a 4cm/1½in round pastry cutter with a little oil to prevent it from sticking, then cut out 24 discs of jelly and put them on top of the sponges.

Put the chocolate in a large heatproof bowl and rest it over a saucepan of gently simmering water, making sure the bottom of the bowl does not touch the water. Heat, stirring occasionally, until the chocolate has melted. Leave to cool slightly, then drizzle over the cakes. Leave them to set, then store in an airtight container in the fridge or a cool place.

Custard Drops

PER SERVING:
FAT 3.5G (OF WHICH SATURATES 1.2G)
CALORIES 99KCAL
PREPARATION TIME: 30 MINUTES
COOKING TIME: 15 MINUTES

This is my take on custard creams. Traditionally, these little biscuits are made with custard powder and would be sandwiched together with a rich butter cream, but the indent in the top of these biscuits means you can fill them with a thick vanilla custard instead.

Preheat the oven to 180°C/350°F/Gas 4 and line two baking trays with baking paper.

Put the flour in a large bowl, then rub in the butter, using your fingertips, until the mixture resembles coarse breadcrumbs. Stir in the sugar and custard powder. Mix together the milk and vanilla bean paste, then pour three-quarters of the liquid into the flour mixture. Stir to mix to a ball of dough, adding the remaining milk if the mixture will not bind together.

With lightly floured hands, divide the dough into 24 equal-sized pieces and roll into balls. Put them on the prepared baking trays, leaving a small gap between each one, and use a floured thumb to press down in the centre of each ball to create a dent in the middle. Bake for 15 minutes until golden and beginning to become firm to the touch, then transfer to a wire rack to cool.

Meanwhile, make the filling. Mix together the custard powder and sugar in a bowl and gradually work in 1 tablespoon of the milk to make a thick paste. Put the remaining milk and the vanilla bean paste in a small saucepan over a low heat until lukewarm. Pour the warm milk over the custard powder paste, mixing all the time. Pour the mixture back into the saucepan and return to a low heat. Bring gently to the boil, stirring all the time, then

Makes 24 biscuits (12 servings)

FOR THE CUSTARD BISCUITS:
100g/3½oz/heaped ¾ cup plain flour
40g/1½oz butter
50g/1¾oz/scant ¼ cup caster sugar
50g/1¾oz/scant ½ cup custard powder
3 tbsp skimmed milk
1 tsp vanilla bean paste

FOR THE CUSTARD CREAM:
2 tbsp custard powder
1 tbsp caster sugar
125ml/4fl oz/½ cup skimmed milk
1 tsp vanilla bean paste

 7 days

boil for 1 minute, still stirring. Pour into a bowl, cover the surface with cling film, to prevent a skin from forming, then leave to cool and set.

Spoon the set custard into a piping bag fitted with a small nozzle. Pipe the custard into the indents in the centre of each biscuit.

Cranberry & Mixed Spice Digestives

PER SERVING:
FAT 4G (OF WHICH SATURATES 2G)
CALORIES 107KCAL
PREPARATION TIME: 15 MINUTES
COOKING TIME: 12 MINUTES

Digestive biscuits have their crumbs in both camps, savoury and sweet. They are perfect with a naughty bit of cheese at the end of a meal or for some dunking action in your tea. This recipe makes no exceptions – they are perfect both ways.

Preheat the oven to 180°C/350°F/Gas 4 and line a baking tray with baking paper.

Mix together the flour, oatmeal, spice and sugar in a bowl. Rub in the butter, using your fingertips, until the mixture resembles coarse breadcrumbs, then stir in the bicarbonate of soda and salt. Stir in the vinegar and cranberries, then finally stir in the milk and mix to a soft dough.

Roll the dough out on a lightly floured surface until it is 5mm/¼in thick. Use a 6cm/2½in round pastry cutter to cut out 24 biscuits. Put the biscuits on the prepared baking tray and bake for 10–12 minutes until lightly golden and firm. Leave to cool on the tray for 2 minutes, then transfer to a wire rack to cool completely. Then you can get dunking!

Makes 24 biscuits (12 servings)

115g/4oz/¾ cup wholemeal flour,
    plus extra for dusting
115g/4oz/scant 1 cup medium oatmeal
1 tsp mixed spice
1 tbsp light soft brown sugar
40g/1½oz cold butter, diced
½ tsp bicarbonate of soda
a pinch of fine sea salt
½ tsp malt vinegar
30g/1oz/¼ cup dried cranberries,
    finely chopped
5 tbsp semi skimmed milk

 7 days

Gingersnap Biscuits

PER SERVING:
  FAT 3G (OF WHICH SATURATES 1G)
  CALORIES 109KCAL
PREPARATION TIME: 15 MINUTES
COOKING TIME: 18 MINUTES

The name says it all really – crunchy little biscuits that add a touch of spice to coffee time.

Preheat the oven to 180°C/350°F/Gas 4 and line two baking trays with baking paper.

Put the butter, syrup and sugar in a small saucepan over a low heat until the butter has melted. Mix together the flour and ground ginger in a large bowl. Add the wet ingredients to the dry ingredients and mix together well.

With damp hands, roll teaspoonfuls of the mixture into balls, then put on the prepared baking trays, leaving a 5cm/2in gap between each one to allow them to spread. You should have 24 biscuits in all. Press them down lightly, then sprinkle over the chopped ginger.

Bake for 12–15 minutes until golden brown. Leave to cool on the tray for 2 minutes, then use a palette knife to transfer to a wire rack to cool completely.

Makes 24 biscuits (12 servings)

50g/1¾oz butter
4 tbsp golden syrup
50g/1¾oz/heaped ¼ cup dark soft brown sugar
180g/6¼oz/1½ cups self-raising flour
2 tsp ground ginger
1 ball of stem ginger, finely chopped

 10 days

Sour Cherry & Almond Cantuccini

PER SERVING:
FAT 3.6G (OF WHICH SATURATES 0.5G)
CALORIES 183KCAL
PREPARATION TIME: 10 MINUTES
COOKING TIME: 40 MINUTES

Cantuccini literally translates as 'coffee bread', as Italians traditionally dip these twice-baked treats into their coffee, so the biscuits soften beautifully as they soak up the liquid. You can easily change the nuts and dried fruit to suit your own taste. If you store them in an airtight container, you can enjoy them for weeks to come.

Preheat the oven to 180°C/350°F/Gas 4 and line two large baking trays with baking paper.

Mix together the flour, sugar and baking powder in a large bowl. Stir in the milk, almonds, sour cherries and eggs, then mix everything together well to form a soft dough.

Turn the dough out onto a lightly floured work surface and divide in half. Shape each piece into a sausage shape 20cm/8in long and put on the prepared baking trays, then press the tops down lightly. Bake for 30 minutes, then remove them from the oven and turn the oven down to 150°C/300°F/Gas 2.

Cut each piece into 12 biscuits about 2cm/¾in thick, using a serrated knife, then put the biscotti back on the baking trays, flat-side up, and bake for a further 10 minutes to dry out completely. Transfer to a wire rack to cool.

Makes 24 biscuits (12 servings)

280g/10oz/2¼ cups plain flour,
    plus extra for dusting
150g/5½oz/⅔ cup caster sugar
1 tsp baking powder
1 tbsp skimmed milk
50g/1¾oz/⅓ cup whole blanched almonds,
    roughly chopped
50g/1¾oz/scant ½ cup dried sour cherries
3 eggs, beaten

 3 weeks

Classic Soft Amaretti

PER SERVING:
FAT 6G (OF WHICH SATURATES 1G)
CALORIES 124KCAL
PREPARATION TIME: 10 MINUTES
COOKING TIME: 12 MINUTES

There are two types of amaretti: Saronno and Morbidi. Amaretti di Saronno are the hard, crunchy biscuits that are perfect for crumbling over trifles and ice cream but Amaretti di Morbidi are the soft, chewy ones made from a meringue base. Morbidi are my favourite and perfect served with a cup of strong coffee.

Preheat the oven to 180°C/350°F/Gas 4 and line two large baking trays with baking paper.

In a clean bowl, whisk the egg whites, using an electric mixer, until stiff peaks form. Gently fold in the sugar and ground almonds, then fold in the almond extract until the ingredients are just combined and you have a smooth paste – do not overmix.

Spoon about 24 teaspoonfuls of the mixture about the size of a small walnut onto the prepared baking trays, leaving a 2.5cm/1in space between them to allow them to spread, then bake for 10–12 minutes until golden brown. Transfer to a wire rack to cool. Dust with a little sifted icing sugar before serving, if you like.

Makes 24 biscuits (12 servings)

a little butter, for greasing
2 egg whites
125g/4½oz/heaped ½ cup caster sugar
125g/4½oz/1¼ cups ground almonds
½ tsp almond extract
a little icing sugar, sifted, for dusting (optional)

 3 weeks

Saffron Biscotti

PER SERVING:
    FAT 4G (OF WHICH SATURATES 0.5G)
    CALORIES 174KCAL
PREPARATION TIME: 10 MINUTES
COOKING TIME: 40 MINUTES

The name for these Italian-style biscuits comes from the Latin word *biscoctus*, which means 'twice baked'. These twice-baked biscuits were a staple of the legions of the Roman army because they keep so well, making them perfect for baking in big batches and storing in airtight containers. Now that your history lesson is over – let's get baking.

Preheat the oven to 180°C/350°F/Gas 4. Put the milk and saffron in a small bowl and leave to soak for 5 minutes.

Mix together the flour, sugar and baking powder in a large bowl. Add the hazelnuts, eggs and the saffron strands and their soaking liquid, then mix everything together to form a dough.

Turn the dough out on a lightly floured work surface and divide in half. Shape each piece into a sausage shape 20cm/8in long and put on two non-stick baking trays, then press the tops down lightly. Bake for 30 minutes, then remove them from the oven and turn the oven down to 150°C/300°F/Gas 2.

Cut each piece into 12 biscuits about 2cm/¾in thick, using a serrated knife, then put the biscotti back on the baking trays, flat-side up, and bake for a further 10 minutes to dry out completely. Transfer to a wire rack to cool.

Makes 24 biscuits (12 servings)

2 tbsp skimmed milk
a pinch of saffron strands
280g/10oz/2¼ cups plain flour,
    plus extra for dusting
150g/5½oz/⅔ cup caster sugar
1 tsp baking powder
50g/1¾oz/⅓ cup skinned whole hazelnuts
3 eggs, beaten

 3 weeks

Florentines

PER SERVING:
 FAT 5.2G (OF WHICH SATURATES 2.7G)
 CALORIES 133KCAL
PREPARATION TIME: 20 MINUTES
COOKING TIME: 15 MINUTES

These are a twist on a classic Florentine. I have cut down the quantity of flaked almonds and replaced them with oats, which are much lower in fat and calories. They are slightly chewier than normal but I love the texture and the flavour – they are like butterscotch: oaty, almondy chews with bursts of fruit and a citrus tang.

Preheat the oven to 170°C/325°F/Gas 3 and line two baking trays with baking paper.

Put the butter, sugar and flour in saucepan over a low heat for a few minutes until the butter has melted. Remove from the heat and gradually add the crème fraîche, stirring continuously until blended. Add the flaked almonds, oats, candied peel, apricots and cherries and mix together well.

Put about 24 teaspoonfuls of the mixture on the prepared baking trays, leaving a 4cm/1½in space between the spoonfuls to allow them to spread, then bake for 10–12 minutes until golden brown. Leave to cool on the baking trays for 5 minutes, then transfer to a wire rack and carefully lift the rack onto the paper-covered baking tray.

Meanwhile, put the chocolate in a large heatproof bowl and rest it over a pan of gently simmering water, making sure the bottom of the bowl does not touch the water. Heat, stirring occasionally, until the chocolate has melted. Use a spoon to drizzle the Florentines with the chocolate. (You'll catch any drips on the baking paper.) Leave to cool and set before serving.

Makes 24 biscuits (12 servings)

30g/1oz butter
75g/2½oz/⅓ cup caster sugar
2 tbsp plain flour
3 tbsp low-fat crème fraîche
30g/1oz/¼ cup flaked almonds
30g/1oz/¼ cup rolled oats
2 tbsp candied peel
50g/1¾oz/heaped ¼ cup dried apricots, finely chopped
40g/1½oz/⅓ cup dried cherries or cranberries, halved
50g/1¾oz dark chocolate, 70% cocoa solids

 3 days   ❄ 3 months

Pistachio & Lemon Thyme Kisses

PER SERVING:
FAT 4.6G (OF WHICH SATURATES 0.5G)
CALORIES 109KCAL
PREPARATION TIME: 10 MINUTES
COOKING TIME: 12 MINUTES

Lemon thyme is totally different from standard thyme. It has a sweet note that is perfect for baking and goes beautifully with pistachios.

Preheat the oven to 180°C/350°F/Gas 4 and lightly grease a baking tray or line with baking paper.

Put the pistachios in a blender and pulse to blend until fine. In a clean bowl, whisk the egg whites, using an electric mixer, until stiff peaks form. Gradually add the sugar, ground pistachios and lemon thyme leaves and continue whisking until you have a smooth paste – do not overmix.

Fit a piping bag with a 2cm/¾in plain or star nozzle, then carefully spoon the mixture into the bag. Be as light-handed as possible as you do not want to knock out any air from the mixture. Pipe the mixture onto the prepared trays, trying to get little points on the tops. (If you do not have a piping bag, use a spoon to put the mixture onto the tray.) Bake for about 10–12 minutes until lightly golden. Transfer to a wire rack to cool, then lightly dust with a little icing sugar to serve.

Makes 24 biscuits (12 servings)

a little butter, for greasing (optional)
125g/4½oz/scant 1 cup shelled pistachio nuts
2 egg whites
125g/4½oz/heaped ½ cup caster sugar
1 tsp lemon thyme leaves
1 tbsp icing sugar, sifted, for dusting

 3 days

Jammy Dodgers

PER SERVING:
   FAT 3.6G (OF WHICH SATURATES 2.2G)
   CALORIES 122KCAL
PREPARATION TIME: 30 MINUTES, PLUS
   20 MINUTES CHILLING
COOKING TIME: 12 MINUTES

I never really understood why some shop-bought makes of Jammy Dodgers have smiley faces stamped into them ... as if we need any encouragement to eat them!

Put the honey, milk and butter in a small saucepan over a low heat until the butter has melted. Mix together the flour, baking powder, cream of tartar and granulated sugar in a bowl, pour over the butter mixture and mix everything together to form a soft dough. Roll the dough out on a piece of baking paper until it is about 1cm/½in thick, then slide it onto a baking tray, cover with cling film and chill for 20 minutes.

Preheat the oven to 180°C/350°F/Gas 4 and line two baking trays with baking paper.

Roll out the dough on a lightly floured work surface to 3mm/⅛in thick and use a 5.5cm/2¼in round pastry cutter to cut out 48 cookies. Put 24 of them on one baking tray. Use a 2.5cm/1in round pastry cutter or small heart-shaped or star-shaped pastry cutter to cut out the centres of the remaining 24 cookies, then put these on the second baking tray. Bake for 8–10 minutes until lightly brown. Transfer to a wire rack to cool.

Put ½ teaspoon of the jam in the centre of the 24 whole cookies. Sift a little icing sugar over the top of the cut-out cookies, then place them on top of the jam and press down lightly.

Makes 24 biscuits (12 servings)

3 tbsp clear honey
2 tbsp skimmed milk
50g/1¾oz butter
200g/7oz/scant 1⅔ cups plain flour,
   plus extra for dusting
½ tsp baking powder
½ tsp cream of tartar
60g/2¼oz/¼ cup granulated sugar
4 tbsp low-sugar raspberry, apricot or
   blackcurrant jam
1 tbsp icing sugar, sifted, for dusting

 7 days 3 months for uncooked dough

Bourbon Biscuits

PER SERVING:
   FAT 3.2G (OF WHICH SATURATES 1.8G)
   CALORIES 106CAL
PREPARATION TIME: 25 MINUTES, PLUS
   10 MINUTES CHILLING
COOKING TIME: 10 MINUTES

To me, bourbon biscuits scream the 90s. They were everywhere and in every household biscuit tin. Not overly sweet, with a slight savoury note of chocolate (I sound like a wine critic now!), they were – and still are – very moreish. They are my Oreo cookie when it comes to the ritual of eating them: top biscuit off, bite off the cream, then devour the bottom biscuit. I'm afraid it's not particularly ladylike but it just has to be done!

Preheat the oven to 160°C/315°F/Gas 2½.

Beat together the butter and sugar in a large bowl, using an electric mixer, until light and creamy, then mix in the milk. Stir in the flour, cornflour, cocoa powder and baking powder and mix everything together really well until you have a stiff paste. Wrap the paste in cling film and chill in the fridge for 10 minutes.

Turn out the paste onto a lightly floured work surface and roll out to 3mm/⅛in thick, about the size that will fit on two non-stick baking trays (this saves you from handling them too much). Use a rectangular pastry cutter or a knife and a ruler to cut out 48 rectangles about 2 x 4cm/¾ x 1½in each, re-rolling any off-cuts if necessary, and put them on the prepared baking trays. If you like, you can decorate half the biscuits with small indentations using the end of a skewer. Sprinkle with a tiny amount of caster sugar, then bake for 8–10 minutes until just firm to the touch and dry, rather than shiny, on top. Carefully transfer to a wire rack to cool.

Meanwhile, to make the filling, put the evaporated milk, coffee essence and cocoa powder in a

Makes 24 biscuits (12 servings)

FOR THE CHOCOLATE BISCUITS:
40g/1½oz butter, softened
50g/1¾oz/scant ¼ cup golden caster sugar,
   plus 1 tsp extra for sprinkling
1 tbsp skimmed milk
100g/3½oz/heaped ¾ cup plain flour,
   plus extra for dusting
1 tbsp cornflour
3 tbsp cocoa powder, sifted
½ tsp baking powder

FOR THE CHOCOLATE FILLING:
2 tbsp evaporated milk
1 tbsp coffee essence
1 tbsp cocoa powder, sifted
75g/2½oz/scant ⅔ cup icing sugar, sifted

 7 days

saucepan over a low heat for a few minutes, stirring occasionally, until melted and combined. Beat in the icing sugar until you have a thick paste, then leave to cool to room temperature.

Spoon the cool filling into a plastic piping bag. Take the undecorated biscuits, as these will be your base, and squeeze a small line of the filling mixture down the centre of each one, taking care not to go right to the ends. Put a decorated biscuit on top of each one and press down lightly to spread the filling, then leave to set.

Cocoa & Wholegrain Cookies

PER SERVING:
    FAT 5.6G (OF WHICH SATURATES 3.2G)
    CALORIES 157KCAL
PREPARATION TIME: 15 MINUTES
COOKING TIME: 12 MINUTES

I got this recipe idea from a semi-sweet biscuit I picked up in Italy while shooting a TV show out there. It's slightly sweet, very cocoa-y (if that's a word!) and nutty from all the wholegrains. I know granary flour is used to make bread but it has all those amazing wholegrains already in it that go perfectly in these cookies.

Preheat the oven to 180°C/350°F/Gas 4 and line two baking trays with baking paper.

Beat together the butter and sugar, using an electric mixer, until light and creamy, then beat in the vanilla extract and the eggs, one at a time. In a separate bowl, mix together the cocoa powder, flour, cornflour, baking powder, bicarbonate of soda and salt. Pour the wet ingredients into the dry ingredients and mix until you form a stiff dough. Add a little milk if the dough is too dry.

Put 24 teaspoonfuls of the mix, about the size of a walnut, on the prepared baking trays, leaving a 2cm/¾in a gap between each one. Bake for 10–12 minutes until starting to firm around the outside. You want them still to be soft in the centre. Leave to cool on the tray for 2 minutes, then carefully transfer to a wire rack to cool completely.

Makes 24 biscuits (12 servings)

50g/1¾oz butter, softened
75g/2½oz/heaped ⅓ cup light soft brown sugar
2 tsp vanilla extract
2 eggs
90g/3¼oz/1 cup cocoa powder
200g/7oz/scant 1⅓ cups granary flour
1 tbsp cornflour
1 tsp baking powder
1 tsp bicarbonate of soda
a pinch of fine sea salt
a little milk (optional)

 6 days

Chocolate Chip & Raisin Cookies

PER SERVING:
   FAT 4.1G (OF WHICH SATURATES 1G)
   CALORIES 144KCAL
PREPARATION TIME: 15 MINUTES
COOKING TIME: 12 MINUTES

Biscuits are quite difficult to make without lots of butter because it is the butter in the dough that gives them their texture. However, the addition of ricotta and oats make these into chewy cookies with a little chocolate and fruit burst to top it off. The fruitiness of the raisins adds sweetness to the dark chocolate and the wholemeal flour means that they actually fill you up, too.

Preheat the oven to 160°C/315°F/Gas 2½ and line two baking trays with baking paper.

Mix together the oats, cinnamon, both the flours and the baking powder in a bowl. In a separate bowl, whisk together the oil, ricotta, sugar and eggs. Add the wet ingredients to the dry ingredients and mix together well. Stir in the chocolate chips and raisins, then mix again.

Put about 24 teaspoonfuls of the mixture on the prepared baking trays, leaving a 2cm/¾in gap between each one, and bake for 10–12 minutes until golden brown and firm to the touch. Leave to cool on the trays for 2 minutes, then carefully transfer to a wire rack to cool completely.

Makes 24 cookies (12 servings)

50g/1¾oz/½ cup rolled oats
1 tsp ground cinnamon
100g/3½oz/⅔ cup wholemeal flour
50g/1¾oz/heaped ⅓ cup plain flour
1 tsp baking powder
2 tbsp canola or coconut oil, melted
50g/1¾oz ricotta cheese
100g/3½oz/heaped ½ cup light soft brown sugar
2 eggs, beaten
50g/1¾oz dark chocolate chips
50g/1¾oz/heaped ⅓ cup raisins

 2 days

Oat & Coconut Cookies

PER SERVING:
FAT 6G (OF WHICH SATURATES 4.4G)
CALORIES 275KCAL
PREPARATION TIME: 15 MINUTES
COOKING TIME: 18 MINUTES

Some cookies are meant to be hard and crunchy but these little bites are soft and chewy because the coconut keeps them moist and makes them a sticky and delicious treat.

Preheat the oven to 180°C/350°F/Gas 4 and line two baking trays with baking paper.

Put the butter, syrup and 3 tablespoons water in a small saucepan over a low heat until the butter has melted. Mix together the flour, coconut, oats, sugar and ginger in a large bowl. Pour in the melted butter and the milk and mix to a dough.

Turn the dough out onto a lightly floured work surface and roll into 24 balls, then put them on the prepared baking trays and lightly press down to flatten them slightly. Bake for 12–15 minutes until light golden brown. Leave to cool on the trays for 2 minutes, then transfer to a wire rack to cool completely.

Makes 24 biscuits (12 servings)

30g/1oz butter
6 tbsp golden syrup
150g/5½oz/1¼ cups plain flour,
    plus extra for dusting
40g/1½oz/½ cup desiccated coconut
250g/9oz/2 ½ cups rolled oats
140g/5oz/scant ⅔ cup caster sugar
1 tsp ground ginger
4 tbsp skimmed milk

 6 days

Traybakes

Treats to share – whichever way you slice them

That is a motto I hold close to my heart. When I get stressed, I bake, and don't my friends and neighbours know it. For me, it often isn't even for the end result, it's more about the process. There is something about being distracted, weighing ingredients, using a bit of elbow grease for mixing and then the calming effect of the fabulous smells wafting from the oven. It's my form of therapy. However, even if the end result wasn't important at the beginning, it soon becomes crucial once something delicious emerges from the oven.

Traybakes are great for pleasing a crowd. They are easy to make and in one batch you have 24 cakes or bars ready to go. If you don't have a rectangular cake tin, you can always use the same size roasting tin or ovenproof dish, just line it with baking paper.

Traybakes are so versatile as you can serve oaty ones for breakfast on the run for the whole family, top fruity ones with a spoonful of yogurt for dessert, and enjoy all kinds for family teas or parties. The world is your oyster when it comes to flavour, so if you have blackberries in the fridge instead of blueberries, feel free to substitute to make the recipes your own.

Raspberry Battenburg-esque Cakes

PER SERVING:
FAT 4G (OF WHICH SATURATES 1G)
CALORIES 171KCAL
PREPARATION TIME: 20 MINUTES
COOKING TIME: 30 MINUTES

A family friend came for Easter one year and brought a delicious, sticky almond cake but when I politely asked for the recipe I was met with a stern, 'no'. It was her signature recipe and she would not give it up. I have to say, I was slightly cross, so I went into the kitchen and made my own version – and this is it. The best part of the story is that a few months later she asked for my recipe as it was 'so delicious'. Of course, I graciously handed it over.

Preheat the oven to 180°C/350°F/Gas 4 and line a 30 x 20cm/12 x 8in cake tin with baking paper. Roll out the marzipan on a work surface lightly dusted with icing sugar into a rectangle about 30 x 20cm/12 x 8in and leave to one side.

Put the eggs, sugar, milk, oil and vanilla extract in a bowl and whisk for 5 minutes, using an electric mixer, until light and creamy. Beat in the apple purée, then beat in the mashed bananas, using a fork. Add the flour, baking powder, bicarbonate of soda and salt and fold everything together.

Divide the mixture in half. Stir the almond extract into one half and fold the raspberries and a few drops of pink food colouring into the other half. Spoon the raspberry mixture into the prepared cake tin, then gently lay the sheet of marzipan on top, pressing down lightly. Spoon the almond cake mixture on top and scatter with the flaked almonds, then bake for 30 minutes until a skewer inserted in the centre comes out clean. Leave to cool in the tin for 30 minutes, then transfer to a wire rack to cool.

Warm the amaretto and agave syrup in a small saucepan, brush over the top of the cooled cake and leave to soak in. Cut into 24 squares to serve.

Makes a 30 x 20cm/12 x 8in cake (24 servings)

250g/9oz golden marzipan
a little icing sugar, sifted, for dusting
3 eggs
300g/10½oz/scant 1⅓ cups caster sugar
150ml/5fl oz/scant ⅔ cup skimmed milk
3 tbsp sunflower oil
2 tbsp vanilla extract
8 tbsp Apple Purée (see page 15)
2 very ripe bananas, mashed
450g/1lb/scant 3⅔ cups plain flour
1 tbsp baking powder
2 tsp bicarbonate of soda
1 tsp fine sea salt
1 tsp almond extract
200g/7oz/scant 1⅔ cups raspberries
a few drops of pink food colouring
30g/1oz/¼ cup flaked almonds
2 tbsp amaretto
1 tbsp agave syrup

 5 days 1 month

Lemon & Blueberry Drizzle Traybake

PER SERVING:
    FAT 2G (OF WHICH SATURATES 1G)
    CALORIES 130KCAL
PREPARATION TIME: 25 MINUTES
COOKING TIME: 35 MINUTES

As the saying goes, 'If it ain't broke, don't fix it.' Well, when it comes to a classic lemon drizzle cake, the classic recipe certainly isn't broken. This version just has the addition of blueberries, which create extra little bursts of fruity flavour. The cake is really sticky and moist so it is best eaten with a fork or you'll end up with very sticky fingers.

Preheat the oven to 180°C/350°F/Gas 4 and line a 30 x 20cm/12 x 8in cake tin with baking paper.

Beat together the butter and sugar in a large bowl, using an electric mixer, until light and creamy. Add the eggs, flour, baking powder, bicarbonate of soda, lemon zest and yogurt and mix everything together well. Fold in the blueberries.

Spoon the mixture into the prepared cake tin and smooth the top a little. Bake for 30–35 minutes until a skewer inserted in the centre comes out clean.

Meanwhile, to make the drizzle, warm the lemon juice in a small saucepan. Put the icing sugar in a bowl and gradually stir in the lemon juice until well blended. Pour over the cooked cake and leave to cool in the tin for 5 minutes, then transfer to a wire rack to cool completely. Cut into 24 squares to serve.

Makes a 30 x 20cm/12 x 8in cake (24 servings)

FOR THE CAKE:
50g/1¾oz butter
200g/7oz/heaped ¾ cup caster sugar
3 eggs
300g/10½oz/heaped 2⅓ cups self-raising flour
1 tsp baking powder
1 tsp bicarbonate of soda
grated zest of 2 lemons
100g/3½oz/scant ½ cup fat-free natural yogurt
150g/5½oz/1 cup blueberries

FOR THE DRIZZLE:
juice of 2 lemons
100g/3½oz/heaped ¾ cup icing sugar, sifted

 3 days

Fruity Flapjacks

PER SERVING:
   FAT 6G (OF WHICH SATURATES 2G)
   CALORIES 195KCAL
PREPARATION TIME: 15 MINUTES
COOKING TIME: 40 MINUTES

Some people like their flapjacks crunchy but I love them when they are super chewy – and these are just that. The little bursts of dried fruit scattered through the mix bring them alive.

Preheat the oven to 180°C/350°F/Gas 4 and line a 30 x 20cm/12 x 8in cake tin with baking paper.

Put the bananas, melted butter, sugar, cinnamon and dates in a food processer and blend until smooth, adding a splash of water if the mixture is very thick. Reserve a handful of the cranberries and sunflower seeds, then mix the remainder with the oats and dried fruits in a large bowl. Pour in the banana mixture and mix well.

Spoon the mixture into the prepared cake tin and press everything down, then scatter the reserved cranberries and sunflower seeds on top and press in lightly. Bake for 35–40 minutes until golden brown. Leave to cool for 10 minutes, then cut into 24 squares while still warm and transfer to a wire rack to cool completely.

Makes a 30 x 20cm/12 x 8in cake (24 servings)

3 medium or 2 large bananas
50g/1¾oz butter, melted
50g/1¾oz/¼ cup dark soft brown sugar
2 tsp ground cinnamon
200g/7oz/scant 1¼ cups pitted dates, roughly chopped
100g/3½oz/¾ cup dried cranberries
150g/5½oz/1¼ cups sunflower seeds
400g/14oz/4 cups rolled oats
100g/3½oz/heaped ¾ cup raisins
100g/3½oz/heaped ½ cup dried apricots, chopped

 7 days 3 months

Crunchy Granola Bars

PER SERVING:
  FAT 5.2G (OF WHICH SATURATES 2.4G)
  CALORIES 169KCAL
PREPARATION TIME: 15 MINUTES
COOKING TIME: 40 MINUTES

These bars require a little more effort than an ordinary granola or cereal bar as the oats are baked before you make the bars, which makes them really crunchy and perfect to give you plenty of energy when you are on the go.

Preheat the oven 180°C/350°F/Gas 4 and line a 30 x 20cm/12 x 8in tin with baking paper.

Put the oats in a large bowl and stir in the melted butter. Spread the oats out on a baking tray and bake for 15 minutes until golden brown, stirring occasionally to prevent them from burning on the edge. Tip onto a plate and leave to cool.

Turn the oven down to 170°C/325°F/Gas 3. Put the honey, apple juice and molasses in a saucepan over a low heat for a few minutes until warmed through and runny. Stir together the crunchy oats and rice cereal in a large bowl, then pour over the warmed honey mixture and stir well to combine.

Spoon the mixture into the prepared cake tin and press down lightly. Bake for 20–25 minutes until golden brown. Leave to cool in the tin for about 15 minutes, then cut into 24 bars, using a sharp knife. Leave to cool completely before serving.

Makes a 30 x 20cm/12 x 8in cake (24 servings)

500g/1lb 2oz/5 cups rolled oats
100g/3½oz butter, melted
200g/7oz/scant ⅔ cup clear honey
125ml/4fl oz/½ cup apple juice
80g/2¼oz/¼ cup molasses
50g/1¾oz/1½ cups rice cereal

 7 days

Blackberry & Coconut Traybake

PER SERVING:
    FAT 5.9G (OF WHICH SATURATES 4G)
    CALORIES 144KCAL
PREPARATION TIME: 20 MINUTES
COOKING TIME: 35 MINUTES

Like all berries, blackberries are best when they are in season. If they are not in season they can be so sour they make your eyes water. If you want to make this cake when there are no blackberries in the hedgerows, pick up a bag of frozen berries and use those instead – you don't even have to defrost them before use.

Preheat the oven to 180°C/350°F/Gas 4 and line a 30 x 20cm/12 x 8in tin with baking paper.

Mix together the flour, sugar and butter in a bowl, then scrape in the seeds from the vanilla pod. Rub in the butter, using your fingertips, until the mixture resembles coarse breadcrumbs. Stir in half the oats and all the coconut. Reserve 6 large spoonfuls of the mixture and leave to one side. Add the eggs to the remaining mixture and mix until smooth, then add enough of the milk to make a thick batter.

Spoon the mixture into the prepared tin and smooth the top a little. Scatter with the blackberries, sprinkle with the reserved crumb mixture, then scatter with the remaining oats. Bake for 30–35 minutes until golden brown and a skewer inserted in the centre comes out clean. Transfer to a wire rack to cool. Cut into 24 squares to serve.

Makes a 30 x 20cm/12 x 8in cake (24 servings)

250g/9oz/2 cups self-raising flour
200g/7oz/heaped 1 cup light soft brown sugar
100g/3½oz butter
1 vanilla pod, split in half lengthways
100g/3½oz/1 cup rolled oats
100g/3½oz/heaped 1 cup desiccated coconut
2 eggs, beaten
100ml/3½fl oz/scant ½ cup skimmed milk
350g/12oz/2⅓ cups fresh or frozen blackberries

 3 days ❄ 1 month

Jamaican Gingerbread

PER SERVING:
    FAT 4G (OF WHICH SATURATES 2G)
    CALORIES 141KCAL
PREPARATION TIME: 20 MINUTES
COOKING TIME: 30 MINUTES

There is a particular brand of shop-bought Jamaican ginger cake that my dad loves and his local corner shop happens to stock. Whenever my mum is away, a loaf seems to appear in the cupboard. I think he loves it because of its dense, sticky texture and lovely sticky top – so that's the result I achieved with this recipe. If only you can leave it for 24 hours before tucking in, it'll taste even better – it's a challenge but well worth it.

Preheat the oven to 180°C/350°F/Gas 4 and line a 30 x 20cm/12 x 8in tin with baking paper.

Put the butter and sugar in a large bowl and beat together, using an electric mixer, until light and creamy. Beat in the syrup, then the eggs, one at a time, adding 1 tablespoon of flour between each egg. Stir in the remaining flour with the bicarbonate of soda, ginger, cinnamon and carrot and mix well, then stir in the milk.

Spoon the batter into the prepared cake tin and smooth the top a little, then sprinkle with the ginger. Bake for 25–30 minutes until a skewer inserted in the centre comes out clean.

Leave to cool in the tin. If you can resist, turn the cake out and store in an airtight container for at least 24 hours before serving as this makes the top go really sticky. Cut into 24 squares to serve.

Makes a 30 x 20cm/12 x 8in cake (24 servings)

100g/3½oz butter
100g/3½oz/heaped ½ cup dark soft brown sugar
200g/7oz golden syrup
2 eggs
400g/14oz/3¼ cups plain flour
2 tsp bicarbonate of soda
1½ tbsp ground ginger
2 tsp ground cinnamon
1 large carrot, grated
250ml/9fl oz/1 cup skimmed milk
4 balls of preserved stem ginger, finely chopped

 4 days   3 months

Peanut & Jelly Squares

PER SERVING:
FAT 5.8G (OF WHICH SATURATES 2.2G)
CALORIES 114KCAL
PREPARATION TIME: 15 MINUTES
COOKING TIME: 20 MINUTES

This is one for my American friends. It's my take on a peanut butter and jelly sandwich. The old calories wouldn't allow for loads of peanut butter but I have managed to squeeze in a few salted peanuts to make up for it.

Preheat the oven to 180°C/350°F/Gas 4 and line a 30 x 20cm/12 x 8in cake tin with baking paper. Put the raspberries in a bowl and lightly mash with the back of a fork. Leave to one side.

Put the butter and honey in a saucepan over a low heat until the butter has melted. Add the vanilla extract and stir in the oats. Spread half the mixture over the base of the prepared tin and press down firmly. Spread with the jam and then top with the mashed raspberries. Add the peanuts to the remaining oat mixture, then scatter this over the top of the raspberries.

Bake for 15–18 minutes until golden brown. Leave to cool in the tin, then cut into 24 squares to serve.

Makes a 30 x 20cm/12 x 8in cake (24 servings)

225g/8oz/scant 2 cups raspberries
75g/2½oz butter
115g/4oz/½ cup clear honey
1 tsp vanilla extract
350g/12oz/3½ cups rolled oats
3 tbsp low-sugar raspberry jam
50g/1¾oz/⅓ cup salted peanuts, roughly chopped

 6 days

Pumpkin & Cinnamon Blondies

PER SERVING:
   FAT 4G (OF WHICH SATURATES 2G)
   CALORIES 139KCAL
PREPARATION TIME: 15 MINUTES
COOKING TIME: 25 MINUTES

Blondies are white chocolate brownies, but because of the high fat content in white chocolate, my jeans just won't allow it in my diet. Instead, I use pumpkin purée, which you can easily buy in tins in the supermarket, to give that dense squidginess. Americans have been using it for years and it's high time we did to – it's low fat and perfect for baking.

Preheat the oven to 180°C/350°F/Gas 4 and line a 30 x 20cm/12 x 8in tin with baking paper.

Put the butter and sugar in a large bowl and beat together, using an electric mixer, until light and creamy. Beat in the eggs, one at a time, then stir in the pumpkin purée. Add the flour, cinnamon, baking powder and nutmeg and mix well.

Spoon the mixture into the prepared cake tin and smooth the top a little, then bake for 20–25 minutes until just set. Cover with a clean tea towel and leave to cool in the tin. Cut into 24 squares to serve.

Makes a 30 x 20cm/12 x 8in cake (24 servings)

100g/3½oz butter
250g/8oz/1⅓ cups dark soft brown sugar
2 eggs
250g/9oz/1 cup pumpkin purée
400g/14oz/3¼ cups plain flour
1 tbsp ground cinnamon
2 tsp baking powder
1 tsp freshly grated nutmeg

 4 days   3 months

Chocolate & Beetroot Brownies

PER SERVING:
  FAT 5.2G (OF WHICH SATURATES 1.9G)
  CALORIES 129KCAL
PREPARATION TIME: 25 MINUTES
COOKING TIME: 25 MINUTES

I have never been a fan of beetroot and have always thought it tastes like I imagine a worm would taste – earthy! However, everybody has the right to change their mind and I have come to the conclusion that beetroot is the best thing to use in low-fat brownies. There's not a hint of worm – just gorgeous, gooey chocolatiness.

Preheat the oven to 170°C/325°F/Gas 3 and line a 30 x 20cm/12 x 8in cake tin with baking paper.

Put the chocolate in a large heatproof bowl and rest it over a saucepan of gently simmering water, making sure the bottom of the bowl does not touch the water. Heat, stirring occasionally, until the chocolate has melted, then remove the bowl from the heat and leave to cool.

Put the eggs, vanilla extract, agave syrup and sugar in a bowl and whisk, using an electric mixer, until light and creamy. Gently fold in the melted chocolate, then gently fold in the flour, bicarbonate of soda and cocoa powder. Finally, stir in the grated beetroot, oil and milk.

Spoon the mixture into the prepared cake tin and smooth the top. Bake for 20–25 minutes until just set but still slightly soft in the centre. Leave to cool in the tin for 10 minutes, then transfer to a wire rack to cool completely. Cut into 24 squares to serve.

Makes a 30 x 20cm/12 x 8in cake (24 servings)

150g/5½oz dark chocolate, 70% cocoa solids
3 eggs
2 tsp vanilla extract
4 tbsp agave syrup
200g/7oz/heaped 1 cup light soft brown sugar
150g/5½oz/1¼ cups self-raising flour
1 tsp bicarbonate of soda
35g/1¼oz/heaped ⅓ cup cocoa powder, sifted
250g/9oz peeled raw beetroot, finely grated
3 tbsp sunflower oil
100ml/3½fl oz/scant ½ cup milk

 5 days 3 months

Sticky Toffee Traybake

PER SERVING:
FAT 6G (OF WHICH SATURATES 3.2G)
CALORIES 198KCAL
PREPARATION TIME: 30 MINUTES
COOKING TIME: 35 MINUTES

Sticky toffee pudding is my not-so-guilty pleasure. I remember cooking for a private dinner party hosted by a TV food critic and we spent the best part of 30 minutes arguing about what constitutes the perfect sticky toffee. I went for dense, dark and sticky – so it almost sticks to the roof of your mouth – while he chose super-light and fluffy. I am doing it my way, because it's all a matter of taste and I think I'm right!

Preheat the oven to 180°C/350°F/Gas 4 and line a 30 x 20cm/12 x 8in cake tin with baking paper. Put the dates, vanilla, coffee essence and bicarbonate of soda in a food processor and add 350ml/12fl oz/scant 1½ cups boiling water. Blend together, taking extra care because of the steam from the boiling water, until you have a smooth purée.

Put the butter and sugar in a large bowl and beat together, using an electric mixer, until light and creamy. Beat in the eggs one at a time, then fold in the date purée and finally the flour.

Spoon the mixture into the prepared tin and bake for 30 minutes until a skewer inserted in the centre comes out clean. Leave to cool in the tin.

To make the sauce, put the condensed milk, brown sugar and butter in a saucepan over a low heat and heat for 3–4 minutes, stirring, until thick and dark. Leave to cool and thicken slightly, then pour over the cake and cut into 24 squares to serve.

Makes a 30 x 20cm/12 x 8in cake (24 servings)

350g/12oz/2 cups pitted dates
2 tsp vanilla extract
4 tbsp coffee essence
2 tsp bicarbonate of soda
75g/2½oz butter, softened
200g/7oz/heaped ¾ cup caster sugar
4 eggs
400g/14oz/3¼ cups self-raising flour

FOR THE SAUCE:
150ml/5fl oz/scant ⅔ cup light condensed milk
100g/3½oz/heaped ½ cup dark soft brown sugar
50g/1¾oz butter

 5 days 2 months

Mocha Squares

PER SERVING:
FAT 6G (OF WHICH SATURATES 4G)
CALORIES 149KCAL
PREPARATION TIME: 30 MINUTES
COOKING TIME: 30 MINUTES

Although I have given up drinking coffee because I realized I was drinking far too much, I still love the flavour so I haven't given it up all together. Now I get my cappuccino hit in cake form. It's a win-win in my book.

Preheat the oven to 180°C/350°F/Gas 4 and line a 30 x 20cm/12 x 8in cake tin with baking paper.

Put the butter, cocoa powder, sugars and coffee in a saucepan over a medium heat and bring to the boil. Turn the heat down to low and simmer for 1 minute, then remove from the heat. Whisk together the milk and eggs. Whisk the flour, baking powder and bicarbonate of soda into the melted butter and sugar mixture, followed by the egg and milk mixture.

Spoon the mixture into the prepared tin and smooth the top a little. Bake for 20–25 minutes until a skewer inserted in the centre comes out clean. Turn the cake out of the tin and transfer to a wire rack to cool.

Mix together the cream cheese and icing sugar. Spread over the cooled cake, then dust with a little cocoa powder. Cut into 24 squares to serve.

Makes a 30 x 20cm/12 x 8in cake (24 servings)

100g/3½oz butter
40g/1½oz/scant ½ cup cocoa powder, sifted
100g/3½oz/heaped ½ cup dark soft brown sugar
100g/3½oz/scant ½ cup caster sugar
200ml/7fl oz/scant 1 cup strong coffee
100ml/3½fl oz/scant ½ cup skimmed milk
2 eggs
350g/12oz/heaped 2¾ cups self-raising flour
2 tsp baking powder
1 tsp bicarbonate of soda

FOR THE MOCHA ICING:
200g/7oz light cream cheese
100g/3½oz/heaped ¾ cup icing sugar, sifted
1 tbsp cocoa powder, sifted

 4 days ❄ 3 months without icing

Arabian Honey Cake

PER SERVING:
   FAT 6G (OF WHICH SATURATES 1G)
   CALORIES 168KCAL
PREPARATION TIME: 25 MINUTES
COOKING TIME: 25 MINUTES

I lived out in the Middle East for a while in 2009 and this cake was on every restaurant menu. It's traditionally made with rose water or orange blossom water but if you are not a fan of either of those you can just replace it with a little more vanilla extract.

Preheat the oven to 180°C/350°F/Gas 4 and line a 30 x 20cm/12 x 8in cake tin with baking paper.

Whisk together the sugar, eggs and oil for about 3 minutes, using an electric mixer, until light and creamy to incorporate as much air as possible. Gently fold in the flour, bicarbonate of soda, orange zest and juice and orange blossom water and mix well, then stir in the grated courgette.

Spoon the cake mixture into the prepared tin and smooth the top a little. Bake in the centre of the oven for 20–25 minutes until risen and just firm to the touch, or until a skewer inserted in the centre comes out clean. Leave to cool in the tin.

Meanwhile, to make the syrup, warm the honey, orange juice, orange blossom water and cinnamon in a saucepan, then add the pistachios. Use a skewer to make a few holes in the cake before pouring over the hot syrup. Leave the cake to stand and absorb all the syrup while it cools. Cut into 24 squares to serve.

Makes a 30 x 20cm/12 x 8in cake (24 servings)

150g/5½oz/⅔ cup caster sugar
4 eggs
6 tbsp sunflower oil
400g/14oz/3¼ cups self-raising flour
2 tsp bicarbonate of soda
grated zest and juice of 1 orange
1 tsp orange blossom water
2 courgettes, grated, about 300g/10½oz
   total weight

FOR THE HONEY TOPPING:
100g/3½oz/scant ½ cup clear honey
juice of 1 orange
1 tsp orange blossom water
1 tsp ground cinnamon
75g/2½oz/½ cup shelled pistachio nuts, chopped

 3 days

Tarts & Pies

A sin-free way to lighten up your day

Well, not if they are traditional tarts and pies. The battle over pastry has always been well fought among dieters. Pastry is full of fat and has barely an iota of goodness in it. The problem is that it tastes great and some of our best-known desserts and baked treats are surrounded by it.

Apple pie was a signature dish of my grandmother and her pastry was so short, it melted in your mouth. But when you watched her make it you could see why – butter, and lots of it. My solution is to use ricotta cheese instead in pastry for pies and tarts, which reduces the fat and gives beautifully crispy results. My Guilt-Free Shortcrust Pastry (see page 18) can be adapted for savoury dishes by leaving out the sugar, or, to jazz up your sweet pies and tarts, why not add a little grated lemon or orange zest.

If you do have a dinner party, pies and tarts are perfect to serve as they can be made a day or two in advance and then stored in the fridge, But do watch out for any midnight fridge raiders … you don't want to be a slice short.

Fig & Almond Tarts

PER SERVING:
   FAT 5.5G (OF WHICH SATURATES 2.6G)
   CALORIES 177KCAL
PREPARATION TIME: 25 MINUTES, PLUS
   10 MINUTES CHILLING
COOKING TIME: 20 MINUTES

I think raw figs are amazing but warmed figs are absolutely spectacular – they take on a whole new flavour and texture. However, they do need a little crunch to go with them to balance out the softness and this is where their partner in crime comes into play – almonds.

Preheat the oven to 190°C/375°F/Gas 5 and line two baking trays with baking paper.

Put the puff pastry on a lightly floured surface and use a 9cm/3½in round pastry cutter to cut out 12 discs. They should weigh about 20g/¾oz each. Take a 6cm/2½in round pastry cutter and gently mark a border around each disc, making sure you don't go all the way through. Put them on the prepared baking trays, cover with cling film and chill in the fridge for 10 minutes.

Carefully brush the outside ring with a little beaten egg yolk (reserving the rest for the ricotta mixture) and use a fork to prick all over the inner circle, then bake for 10 minutes.

Meanwhile, put the ricotta in a bowl and stir in the lemon zest, 1 tablespoon of the honey and the remaining egg yolks. Mix everything together well. Remove the pastry discs from the oven and press the centre pieces down, then put 2 spoonfuls of the ricotta mixture into the centre of each disc. Cut a cross in the top of each fig, then put it in the centre of each disc. Bake for a further 10 minutes.

Warm the remaining honey slightly to make it a little runnier, then drizzle it over the tarts and sprinkle with flaked almonds to serve.

Makes 12 tarts (12 servings)

1 sheet of light puff pastry, 35 x 25cm/14 x 10in
a little flour, for dusting
2 egg yolks, beaten
150g/5½oz ricotta cheese
grated zest of ½ lemon
4 tbsp clear honey
12 just-ripe figs
1 tbsp flaked almonds, toasted

Apricot & Rosemary Tart

PER SERVING:
    FAT 4G (OF WHICH SATURATES 2G)
    CALORIES 125KCAL
PREPARATION TIME: 30 MINUTES, PLUS 20
    MINUTES INFUSING AND CHILLING
COOKING TIME: 20 MINUTES

My mum's amazing apricot tart started my love affair with *crème pâtissière* served with tart fruits, so I am particularly pleased with this low-calorie twist on our classic family recipe.

Preheat the oven to 180°C/350°F/Gas 4. Put the milk and half the rosemary sprigs in a saucepan over a low heat, scrape the seeds from the vanilla pod into the milk, then add the pod and heat until just lukewarm. Remove from the heat and leave to infuse for 10 minutes. Discard the rosemary, then lift out, rinse and dry the vanilla pod and put it in a container of sugar to make vanilla sugar.

Mix together the eggs, egg yolks, sugar and cornflour, then gradually whisk in the warm milk. Pour the mixture back into a clean saucepan over a low heat and cook for 3 minutes, stirring continuously, until it starts to thicken. The cornflour will go lumpy at first, but use a whisk and some arm power to get rid of any lumps. Once it starts to bubble, remove from the heat and spoon into a bowl. Cover with cling film on the surface of the custard and leave to cool.

Meanwhile, put the apricot halves in an ovenproof dish, drizzle over the honey, then add the remaining rosemary sprigs and the orange juice. Roast for 10 minutes until they start to soften, then leave to cool.

While they are cooling, take a 35 x 13 x 3cm/ 14 x 5 x 1¼in non-stick flan tin. Cut the pastry sheets so they are 20cm/8in wide, keeping the sheets you are not using covered in a damp tea towel to prevent them from drying out. Brush the filo pastry sheets with a little melted butter (they do not need

Makes a 35 x 13cm/14 x 5in tart (12 servings)

FOR THE CRÈME PÂTISSIÈRE:
300ml/10½fl oz/scant 1¼ cups skimmed milk
4 rosemary sprigs, plus extra for sprinkling
1 vanilla pod, split in half lengthways
2 eggs
2 egg yolks
2 tbsp caster sugar
30g/1oz/¼ cup cornflour

FOR THE APRICOT BASE & TOPPING:
12 apricots, halved and pitted
1 tbsp clear honey
juice of 1 orange or a little apple juice
4 sheets of filo pastry, 34 x 30cm/13½ x 12in each
30g/1oz butter, melted

to be completely covered so concentrate around the edges), then line the base and sides of the tin with the pastry. You don't want any gaps but it doesn't matter if you have to stagger them slightly. Push the pastry carefully into the sides of the tin, then cover with cling film and chill in the fridge for 10 minutes. Bake for 10 minutes until cooked and golden brown, then transfer to a wire rack to cool.

When all three elements are cool, spoon the custard into the pastry case, top with the cooled roasted apricots, drizzle over any roasting juices and sprinkle with a few rosemary leaves.

Cherry Bakewell Tart

PER SERVING:
   FAT 4.4G (OF WHICH SATURATES 1.75G)
   CALORIES 152KCAL
PREPARATION TIME: 25 MINUTES, PLUS 10
   MINUTES CHILLING
COOKING TIME: 50 MINUTES

I can hear the people of Bakewell shouting from here. I know it's not a classic Bakewell tart but when you guys come up with such a great recipe, those of us watching the calories still want to enjoy it. It works equally well with raspberries, plum halves, blueberries or blackberries.

Preheat the oven to 180°C/350°F/Gas 4 and lightly oil a 20cm/8in deep, fluted non-stick tart tin with a little low-calorie cooking oil spray.

To make the pastry, put the flour in a large bowl, then rub in the butter, using your fingertips, until the mixture resembles coarse breadcrumbs. Stir in the sugar, then use a fork to mix in the ricotta and gently blend to a smooth dough, adding up to 1 tablespoon water, if necessary, a drop at a time, to bind the ingredients together. Cover with cling film and chill in the fridge for 10 minutes.

Turn the dough out onto a lightly floured surface and roll out to 3mm/⅛in thick. Use to line the base and sides of the prepared tin. Carefully push the pastry into the flutes of the tin, leaving any overhanging pastry attached. Line the pastry with baking paper and cover with baking beans. Bake for 12 minutes, then remove the paper and beans. Brush the base and sides of the pastry with a little egg white, then bake for a further 10 minutes until golden. Remove from the oven and use a serrated knife to trim off any excess pastry.

Spread the jam over the base of the tart, then sprinkle over the cherry halves. Mix together the ground almonds, polenta, flour and caster sugar. In a separate bowl, whisk together the eggs, yogurt and almond extract. Add the wet ingredients to the

Makes a 20cm/8in tart (12 servings)

FOR THE LOW-FAT SHORTCRUST PASTRY:
low-calorie cooking oil spray, for greasing
150g/5½oz/1¼ cups plain flour, plus extra for dusting
30g/1oz butter, chilled
1 tbsp caster sugar
3 tbsp ricotta cheese
1 egg white

FOR THE CHERRY FILLING & ALMOND TOPPING:
1 tbsp cherry or raspberry jam
200g/7oz/heaped 1½ cups pitted cherries, halved
30g/1oz/¼ cup ground almonds
50g/1¾oz/⅓ cup fine polenta
2 tbsp plain flour
50g/1¾oz/scant ¼ cup caster sugar
2 eggs
150g/5½oz/scant ⅔ cup fat-free natural yogurt
1 tsp almond extract

FOR THE ICING:
1 tbsp icing sugar, sifted

 2 days   1 month

dry ingredients and mix together well. Spoon evenly over the cherries. Bake for 20 minutes until just set with a slight wobble in the centre. Cool in the tin.

Meanwhile, put the icing sugar in a small bowl and add about 1 teaspoon water, a drop at a time, stirring vigorously until you have a thick paste that just runs off a spoon. Drizzle in lines across the tart, then leave to set for 5 minutes before serving.

Plum & Cardamom Tart

PER SERVING:
FAT 4G (OF WHICH SATURATES 2G)
CALORIES 175KCAL
PREPARATION TIME: 40 MINUTES
COOKING TIME: 1 HOUR

By weight, cardamom is one of the world's most expensive spices and, like saffron, you need very little to make a big impact. If you take the seeds out of their papery cases, their flavour becomes super strong. You might know the flavour if you have ever bitten into a whole pod in your treat-night curry. In this recipe, the apple purée is infused with the whole pods to give the dish a subtle warming flavour.

Preheat the oven to 180°C/350°F/Gas 4 and line a 25cm/10in loose-based flan tin with baking paper. Put a baking tray in the oven to heat up (this will help cook the base of the pastry).

To make the pastry, put the flour in a large bowl, then rub in the butter, using your fingertips, until the mixture resembles coarse breadcrumbs. Use a fork to mix in the ricotta and gently blend to a smooth dough, adding enough of the iced water, a drop at a time, to bind the ingredients together. Cover with cling film and chill in the fridge for 10 minutes.

Meanwhile, put the apples, cardamom pods and 4 tablespoons water in a saucepan over a low heat. Cover with a lid, bring to the boil, then simmer gently for 5–10 minutes until really soft. Discard the cardamom pods, then mash the apples to a purée.

Roll out the pastry on a lightly floured work surface until it is 3mm/⅛in thick, then use it to line the prepared flan tin, leaving any overhanging pastry. Line the pastry case with a piece of baking paper and cover with baking beans. Put on the hot baking tray and bake for 15 minutes, then remove the paper and baking beans and bake for a further 5 minutes until just golden. Remove the pastry case from the

Makes a 25cm/10in tart (12 servings)

FOR THE PASTRY:
225g/8oz/heaped 1¾ cups plain flour, plus extra for dusting
35g/1¼oz butter
4 tbsp ricotta cheese
100ml/3½fl oz/scant ½ cup iced cold water

FOR THE PLUM FILLING:
3 large eating apples, such as Pink Lady or Braeburn, peeled, cored and cut into 2cm/¾in chunks
4 cardamom pods
750g/1lb 10oz ripe, but still firm plums, pitted and quartered
2 tbsp smooth plum or apricot jam

 2 days

oven and leave to cool slightly before trimming off any excess pastry, using a serrated knife.

Spoon the apple purée into the base of the pastry case. Starting from the outside, fan the plum quarters around the tart, working your way into the centre. Bake for 30 minutes until the plums are soft.

Transfer to a wire rack to cool. While the tart is cooling, warm the jam in the microwave or in a small saucepan, then brush the top of the tart to give it a nice glaze. Serve cold.

Canterbury Tarts

PER SERVING:
    FAT 6G (OF WHICH SATURATES 3G)
    CALORIES 276KCAL
PREPARATION TIME: 40 MINUTES
COOKING TIME: 25 MINUTES

I first made a version of this tart when I was at cookery school and thought it was delicious and super easy to make. But the best thing about it is that at the same time it is both low fat and a total flavour explosion. All the flavours come from the naturally sweet fruits and not mountains of sugar and butter, and the filling is packed with juicy apple purée. It's a real treat and it feels like it. The filo pastry is a great way to cut the fat without banning pastry altogether, and a portion of my Guilt-Free Frozen Vanilla Yogurt (see page 21) – or a good-quality shop-bought one – is a perfect accompaniment to an apple tart. It is lower in calories and saturated fat than ice cream, although a serving with a Canterbury Tart would have to be a special occasion as it would push the calorie count over the 300 limit.

Preheat the oven to 170°C/325°F/Gas 3 and put a baking tray in the oven to heat up (this will help cook the base of the pastry). Lightly spray a 6-hole tartlet tin with low-calorie cooking oil spray.

Take 1 sheet of filo pastry, keeping the sheets you are not using covered in a damp tea towel to prevent them from drying out. Brush it lightly with one-third of the melted butter, then sprinkle with one-third of the brown sugar. Top this with another 2 sheets of pastry, brushing with butter and sugar as before, then top with the final sheet. Using a saucer or mug to guide you, cut out six 10cm/4in pastry circles. Use the pastry to line the prepared tartlet tins, gently pushing the pastry into the corners of the tins. Cover with cling film and chill in the fridge while you make the filling.

Makes 6 tarts (6 servings)

low-calorie cooking oil spray, for greasing
4 sheets of filo pastry, 34 x 30cm/13½ x 12in each
30g/1oz butter, melted
4 tbsp light soft brown sugar
3 eggs
110g/3¾oz/scant ½ cup caster sugar
3 tbsp Apple Purée (see page 15)
grated zest and juice of 1½ lemons
6 eating apples, cored

  1 month

To make the filling, mix together the eggs, caster sugar, apple purée, lemon zest and juice, then stir in the butter. Grate the unpeeled apples and stir them into the egg mixture, then spoon the mixture into the tartlet cases.

Pop the tarts onto the hot baking tray and bake for about 20–25 minutes, or until the centres of the tarts are just set and the pastry is a light golden brown. Transfer to a wire rack to cool slightly before serving warm.

French Apple Tart

PER SERVING:
FAT 2.2G (OF WHICH SATURATES 1G)
CALORIES 112KCAL
PREPARATION TIME: 25 MINUTES, PLUS
10 MINUTES CHILLING
COOKING TIME: 1 HOUR

This recipe is so simple to whip up when guests pop round unexpectedly. Literally five ingredients and you are away, and nobody would guess it was low in fat. Even the most novice of bakers could attempt this one and come out with a creation that not only looks beautiful, but also tastes great.

To make the apple purée, peel and core 2 of the apples then cut into 1cm/½in dice. Put them in a saucepan with 1 tablespoon water. Bring to the boil over a medium heat, then turn the heat down to low and simmer gently for about 10 minutes until the apples start to break down to a purée, using a fork to help break up any big lumps. Purée with a hand-held blender, or in a blender if you like a very smooth purée. Tip the purée into a bowl and leave to cool. (If you want to miss out this step, you can use about 2 tablespoons shop-bought apple purée.)

Preheat the oven to 180°C/350°F/Gas 4 and line a baking sheet with baking paper.

Give the sheet of puff pastry a couple of rolls on a lightly floured surface to make it a little wider. Take a dinner plate about 25cm/10in in diameter and cut round it to give you a large disc of pastry and put it carefully on a non-stick baking tray. Crimp the edges of the pastry by pressing the edge of the pastry between the index finger of one hand and the thumb and index finger of the other hand to make a scalloped edge. Cover with cling film and chill in the fridge for 10 minutes.

Peel and core the remaining apples, then cut into slices about 3mm/⅛in thick. Remove the pastry from the fridge and spread the apple purée over

Makes a 25cm/10in tart (12 servings)

5 crisp eating apples, such as Braeburn
1 sheet of light puff pastry, about 180g/6¼oz total weight
a little flour, for dusting
2 tbsp clear honey
1 egg, beaten
low-fat crème fraîche or Guilt-Free Frozen Vanilla Yogurt (see page 21), to serve (optional)

 2 days

the base, leaving a 1cm/½in clear border around the edge. Take the sliced apples and, starting from the outside of the tart and working in, fan the slices out to cover the surface of the apple purée. Once the whole tart is covered (apart from the border), drizzle with the honey. Brush the pastry with a little beaten egg, then bake for 30 minutes until the edges are golden brown. Serve warm with low-fat crème fraîche or frozen yogurt, if you like.

Jammy Tarts with Fresh Fruit

PER SERVING:
FAT 5G (OF WHICH SATURATES 2.3G)
CALORIES 175KCAL
PREPARATION TIME: 15 MINUTES
COOKING TIME: 10 MINUTES

I hated jam tarts as a kid. At every birthday party, a box would be produced and the brightly coloured, sticky, sickly sweet, dry, crusted tarts would be handed round – horrid. However, bad memories can create great recipes, although these little jammy treats have only the vaguest resemblance to my childhood memory. You can use blueberries or pitted cherries instead of the raspberries, if you prefer, and any flavour of jam. It's an easy recipe to adapt to make as many tarts as you like.

Preheat the oven to 190°C/375°F/Gas 5.

Take the crust-less slices of bread and use a rolling pin to roll them out until they are really thin. Brush one side of each slice with a little melted butter, then gently press each slice, butter-side out, into the sections of a 6-hole muffin tin. Push the bread right into the sections to create little baskets. Brush the insides with a little beaten egg, then bake for 5 minutes until the bread is golden brown and crisp.

Put 1 teaspoonful of the jam in each bread basket, then put them back in the oven for a further 5 minutes. Carefully transfer the baskets to a wire rack to cool.

When the baskets are cold, spoon in the yogurt, then top with the fresh fruit and serve immediately.

Makes 6 tarts (6 servings)

6 thin slices of white bread, crusts removed
30g/1oz butter, melted
1 egg, beaten
6 tsp low-sugar jam of any flavour
6 tbsp low-fat strawberry yogurt
2 kiwi fruit, peeled and cut into 5mm/¼in half moons
200g/7oz/1⅓ cups strawberries
200g/7oz/scant 1⅔ cups raspberries

Pear Tarts Tatin

PER SERVING:
  FAT 6G (OF WHICH SATURATES 4G)
  CALORIES 258KCAL
PREPARATION TIME: 30 MINUTES
COOKING TIME: 18 MINUTES

We all make mistakes in the kitchen but sometimes those very disasters create legendary new dishes. Tarte Tatin was apparently such a dish, which was the result of two sisters dropping a single-crust apple pie on the floor, fruit-side up. Now however good this classic tart tastes, it is just too naughty for us, so my version combines all the best bits with a little less sin.

Peel the pears, leaving the stalks attached. Cut a small slice off the bottom of each pear so that they stand up easily. Use a melon baller to remove the core by scooping it out from the bottom of the pear. Stand the pears upright in a saucepan so they just fit in the pan. Pour in 1l/35fl oz/4 cups water, then add the lemon zest and juice, cinnamon stick and 2 tablespoons of the sugar. Put the pan over a high heat and bring to the boil, then turn the heat down to low and simmer gently for 5 minutes until the pears are soft when pierced with the tip of a knife. Remove from the heat and leave to cool.

Preheat the oven to 200°C/400°F/Gas 6.

Cut 6 strips from the pastry about 30cm/12in long and 1cm/½in wide. Brush the strips with a little beaten egg. Take a piece of pastry and wrap one end around the top of the first pear, just under the stalk, and press the pastry into itself to seal it and attach it to the pear. Twist the pastry around the pear so it looks like a helter skelter. When you get to the base of the pear, tuck the pastry underneath, so that the weight of the pear keeps it in place, and put the pear in a non-stick baking tray. Repeat with the remaining pears. Bake for 10 minutes until the pastry is golden.

Makes 6 tarts (6 servings)

6 just-ripe pears with stalks
1 lemon, zest removed with a vegetable peeler, then juiced
1 cinnamon stick
5 tbsp caster sugar
100g/3½oz light puff pastry sheets
1 egg, beaten
20g/¾oz butter
4 tbsp condensed milk

Meanwhile, sprinkle the remaining sugar into the base of a non-stick frying pan over a medium heat for a few minutes until it caramelizes and turns golden brown. Remove from the heat and add the butter, stir to combine, then stir in the condensed milk and leave to cool slightly while the pears finish cooking. Serve hot with the caramel sauce.

Light Lemon Meringue Pies

PER SERVING:
FAT 3G (OF WHICH SATURATES 2G)
CALORIES 166KCAL
PREPARATION TIME: 30 MINUTES
COOKING TIME: 50 MINUTES

Sweet meringue and tangy lemon – it's a pie made in heaven, and you'll just love it.

Preheat the oven to 200°C/400°F/Gas 6 and lightly spray a 12-hole bun tin with a little low-calorie cooking oil spray.

To make the pastry, put the flour in a large bowl and rub in the butter, using your fingertips, until the mixture resembles coarse breadcrumbs. Stir in the sugar and lemon zest and then, using a fork, mix in the ricotta and gently blend to a smooth dough, adding up to 1 tablespoon water, if necessary, a drop at a time, to bind the ingredients together.

Roll out the pastry on a lightly floured work surface until 3mm/⅛in thick, then cut out 12 x 6cm/2½in discs. Gently press into the prepared tin, then brush with egg white, cover with cling film and chill in the fridge for 10 minutes while you make the filling.

Make the filling by whisking together the sugar, cornflour and salt in a saucepan, then gradually whisk in 300ml/10½fl oz/scant 1¼ cups water. Bring to the boil over a medium heat, stirring, then turn the heat down to low and simmer for 1 minute.

Whisk together the lemon juice, zest and eggs in a bowl, then stir in a small amount of the hot water mixture. Whisk this back into the water and sugar mixture (this prevents the eggs from splitting). Return the pan to the heat for 30 seconds, then whisk the butter into the mix. Pour this into a bowl, cover the surface with cling film and leave to cool.

In a clean bowl, whisk the egg whites, using an electric mixer, until stiff peaks form. Gradually

Makes 12 pies (12 servings)

FOR THE PASTRY:
low-calorie cooking oil spray, for greasing
150g/5½oz/1¼ cups plain flour, plus extra
    for dusting
30g/1oz butter
1 tbsp caster sugar
grated zest of 1 lemon
3 tbsp ricotta cheese

FOR THE LEMON FILLING:
150g/5½oz/⅔ cup caster sugar
30g/1oz/⅓ cup cornflour
1 tsp salt
125ml/4fl oz/½ cup lemon juice
grated zest of 2 lemons
2 eggs
2 tsp butter

FOR THE MERINGUE:
3 egg whites
50g/1¾oz/scant ¼ cup caster sugar
¼ tsp cream of tartar

 3 days

add the sugar and cream of tartar and continue whisking until thick and glossy.

Spoon 1 tablespoon of lemon curd into the base of each pie. Spoon the meringue into a piping bag with a star nozzle, then pipe the meringue on top of the curd and bake for 12–15 minutes until just browning on the top. Leave to cool before serving.

Chocolate & Raspberry Tart

PER SERVING:
 FAT 6G (OF WHICH SATURATES 3.8G)
 CALORIES 192KCAL
PREPARATION TIME: 20 MINUTES, PLUS MAKING
 THE PASTRY AND 2 HOURS CHILLING
COOKING TIME: 25 MINUTES

Dark chocolate is full of antioxidants so a little bit is considered good for you. And this indulgent chocolate treat is so easy to make and so delicious it's worth its place in the book.

Preheat the oven to 180°C/350°F/Gas 4 and lightly spray a 23cm/9in deep, fluted non-stick tart tin with low-calorie cooking oil spray.

Roll out the pastry on a lightly floured surface to 3mm/⅛in thick. Line the base and sides of the prepared tin, pushing the pastry into the flutes and leaving it overhanging. Cover with cling film and chill for 10 minutes.

Meanwhile, put the chocolate in a large heatproof bowl and rest it over a saucepan of gently simmering water, making sure the bottom of the bowl does not touch the water. Heat, stirring, until the chocolate has melted. Mix together the cocoa powder, milk and vanilla extract. Fold the mixture into the chocolate with 2 tablespoons boiling water. Leave to cool to body temperature.

Line the pastry case with baking paper and cover with baking beans. Bake for 12 minutes, then remove the paper and beans. Brush the pastry with egg white, then bake for a further 10 minutes until golden. Remove from the oven and trim off any excess pastry, using a serrated knife.

In a clean bowl, whisk the egg whites, using an electric mixer, until stiff peaks form. Gradually add the sugar and continue whisking until thick. Fold the crème fraîche into the chocolate. Fold in one-third of the egg whites, then the remainder. Spoon into

Makes a 23cm/9in tart (12 servings)

low-calorie cooking oil spray, for greasing
1 recipe quantity Guilt-Free Shortcrust Pastry
 (see page 18)
a little flour, for dusting
1 egg white

FOR THE CHOCOLATE FILLING:
100g/3½oz/scant 1 cup dark chocolate chips,
 70% cocoa solids
1 tbsp cocoa powder
2 tbsp semi-skimmed milk
2 tsp vanilla extract
2 egg whites
2 tbsp caster sugar
50g/1¾oz/scant ¼ cup low-fat crème fraîche

FOR THE RASPBERRY TOPPING:
400g/14oz/3¼ cups raspberries
1 tbsp icing sugar, sifted

 2 days

the prepared pastry case and smooth the top. Put in the fridge for 2 hours to set. Put the raspberries on top and sprinkle with icing sugar to serve.

Blueberry & White Chocolate Tart

PER SERVING:
    FAT 5G (OF WHICH SATURATES 2.75G)
    CALORIES 130KCAL
PREPARATION TIME: 15 MINUTES, PLUS 40
    MINUTES CHILLING
COOKING TIME: 20 MINUTES

When is comes to lower-fat, lower-calorie recipes, white chocolate is usually a no-go area, but I just love it – for me it's a guilty pleasure, even though I know, as a chef, it is not really chocolate. So I was determined to include it in this book, and the best way to use it if you are watching those all-important numbers is to mix it with something else, like buttermilk, and cut down on the sugar in other areas of the recipe.

Preheat the oven to 200°C/400°F/Gas 6 and line a baking tray with baking paper.

Unroll the pastry on a lightly floured surface and cut into a 30cm/12in square. Put the pastry on the prepared baking tray and mark a 1cm/½in border around the edge with a knife, making sure you don't cut through the pastry. Cover with cling film and chill in the fridge for 10 minutes.

Brush the border with a little of the beaten egg, taking care not to drip it over the edge as this will prevent the pastry from rising. Stab the centre of the pastry repeatedly with a fork – this is known as 'docking' – then bake for 15 minutes until golden brown. The border should have risen up and the centre remained flat, creating a rectangular tart case. Transfer the pastry to a wire rack. If the centre has risen up, gently press it back down. To reduce the calories further, you could remove some pastry layers from the centre, if you like. Leave to cool.

While the pastry is cooling, put the chocolate in a large heatproof bowl and rest it over a pan of gently simmering water, making sure the bottom of the bowl does not touch the water. Heat, stirring occasionally, until the chocolate begins to melt. Turn

Makes a 30cm/12in tart (12 servings)

FOR THE BLUEBERRY TART:
200g/7oz ready-rolled light puff pastry
a little flour, for dusting
1 egg, beaten
75g/2½oz white chocolate, cut into small pieces
600g/1lb 5oz/4 cups blueberries
100ml/3½fl oz/scant ½ cup buttermilk

FOR THE CHOCOLATE TOPPING:
10g/½oz white chocolate (1 square from a bar), grated
a few mint leaves, torn into pieces

off the heat and leave the chocolate to melt in the residual heat. (This will prevent the chocolate from splitting, and white chocolate is prone to this.)

Meanwhile, put 100g/3½oz/⅔ cup of the blueberries in a frying pan with 2 tablespoons water. Bring to the boil over a medium heat, then turn the heat down to low and leave to simmer for about 4 minutes until they start to pop. Purée, using a hand-blender or by transferring to a blender or food processor, then rub through a sieve.

Once the chocolate has melted, gently fold in the buttermilk, then pour the mixture into the tart case and scatter with the remaining blueberries. Chill in the fridge for 30 minutes until set. Just before serving, drizzle the tart with the blueberry sauce, sprinkle with chocolate and scatter with the mint leaves.

Perfect Peach Pies

PER SERVING:
   FAT 6G (OF WHICH SATURATES 4G)
   CALORIES 256KCAL
PREPARATION TIME: 15 MINUTES
COOKING TIME: 15 MINUTES

Peaches are so difficult to find perfectly ripe. Cooking with them brings out their natural flavour so you can use slightly underripe ones for this recipe, although do use the perfectly soft and sweet ones if you can find them. Whichever you use, it's a delicious dessert.

Preheat the oven to 190°C/375°F/Gas 5.

Put the peach halves, cut-side up, in an ovenproof dish. If they do not sit flat, cut a thin slice off the rounded side so that they are steady. Put an amaretti biscuit in the hole of each peach where the pit once was, then add a splash of the amaretto (you can leave this out if you are feeding the kids).

Take 1 half-sheet of filo at a time, keeping the sheets you are not using covered in a damp tea towel to prevent them from drying out. Brush each sheet of filo with a little melted butter (they don't have to be completely covered), then scrunch 1 sheet on top of each peach half.

Squeeze the orange juice into the bottom of the dish and add the remaining amaretto, then bake for 15 minutes until the pastry is crisp and golden and the peaches are soft. Turn upside down onto serving plates and serve with the crème fraîche.

Makes 12 pies (6 servings)

6 large ripe peaches, halved and pitted
12 amaretti biscuits
6 tbsp amaretto (optional)
6 sheets of filo pastry, 34 x 30cm/13½ x 12in each, cut in half
60g/2¼oz butter, melted
juice of 1 large orange
185g/6½oz/¾ cup low-fat crème fraîche, to serve

Pear & Blackberry Pie

PER SERVING:
  FAT 3G (OF WHICH SATURATES 1.75G)
  CALORIES 115KCAL
PREPARATION TIME: 20 MINUTES, PLUS
  30 MINUTES CHILLING
COOKING TIME: 30 MINUTES

My maternal grandmother was the queen of pies. I can generally eat a dish in a restaurant or café and get home and recreate it – it's habit and a skill most chefs pick up. But I just cannot make an apple pie like my grandmother. It's not human nature to admit our shortcomings but this is mine – I can't do it. So I have given up and I now make other pies instead. This one is my favourite and – though I say so myself – it is blinking good!

To make the pastry, put the flour in a large bowl, then rub in the butter, using your fingertips, until the mixture resembles coarse breadcrumbs. Stir in the sugar, then use a fork to break the ricotta into the mix. Add the orange zest, then gradually add about 1 tablespoon water, a drop at a time, and mix to a dough. Add the water very gradually as all flours absorb different amounts of water. Roll the pastry into a ball and flatten to a patty, then wrap in cling film and chill in the fridge for 30 minutes.

While the pastry is chilling, peel, core and slice the pears. Put them in a bowl with the blackberries. Dust with the cornflour and toss everything together, then drizzle over the agave syrup and mix once more.

Preheat the oven to 180°C/350°F/Gas 4 and line a baking tray with baking paper.

Roll out the pastry on a lightly floured surface to a 30cm/12in circle and put it on the prepared baking tray. Scatter the base of the pastry with the semolina – this will help absorb any juices and prevent the pastry from having a soggy base. Pile the fruit in the centre of the pastry and bring the

Makes a 25cm/10in pie (12 servings)

FOR THE RICOTTA PASTRY:
150g/5½oz/1¼ cups plain flour, plus extra for dusting
30g/1oz butter
1 tbsp caster sugar
3 tbsp ricotta cheese
grated zest of 1 orange

FOR THE PEAR & BLACKBERRY FILLING:
4 pears
250g/9oz/2 cups blackberries
1 tbsp cornflour
1 tbsp agave syrup
1 tbsp dried semolina or couscous (bear with me!)
1 egg, beaten
1 tbsp clear honey
juice of 1 orange

sides of the pastry up around the fruit. This doesn't have to be neat – you want it to look rustic. If the pastry does crack, just patch it up. Brush the outside of the pastry with a little beaten egg. Bake for 30 minutes until the fruit has softened but has not gone mushy and the pastry is cooked and golden. Transfer to a wire rack to cool.

Meanwhile, put the honey and orange juice in a small saucepan and bring to the boil over a medium heat. Turn the heat down to low and simmer for about 2 minutes until syrupy. Brush this over the cooked pie before serving.

Spiced Rhubarb Cobbler

PER SERVING:
   FAT 3.7G (OF WHICH SATURATES 1.9G)
   CALORIES 176KCAL
PREPARATION TIME: 20 MINUTES
COOKING TIME: 30 MINUTES

'It will give you tummy ache if you keep eating it like that!' Those were the wise words of my mother as I sat dunking sticks of rhubarb in the sugar pot. Unfortunately, as all mothers are, she was right. Tummy ache was always the consequence of the strange snacking habits of a six-year-old Gee. I still love the tartness of rhubarb and try not to over-sweeten it in desserts, but I have also learnt to wait until it is cooked before eating it. When I was working on a TV show called *Market Kitchen* many years ago, one of the chefs spiced their rhubarb dish with star anise and cinnamon and, although I can't remember who it was, I am using the idea as the starting point for this recipe, so thank you for the idea whoever you were.

Preheat the oven to 180°C/350°F/Gas 4.

Beat together the butter and sugar in a large bowl, using an electric mixer, until light and creamy. Mix in the flours, baking powder and cinnamon, then add the egg and three-quarters of the milk and mix to make a thick batter, adding a little more milk if necessary. You want a thick, sticky batter. You can always add more liquid but it's a little difficult to take it away!

Put the rhubarb in a 25 x 18cm/10 x 7in oval ovenproof dish and pour over the agave syrup. Scrape the seeds from the vanilla pod into the syrup, then add the vanilla pod, star anise, cinnamon stick, cardamom pods and orange zest.

Put the cornflour in a bowl and blend to a paste with the orange juice. Add this to the rhubarb, mix everything together, then spread evenly in the dish.

Makes a 25 x 18cm/10 x 7in oval pie (12 servings)

FOR THE COBBLER TOPPING:
40g/1½oz butter, softened
80g/2¾oz/⅓ cup caster sugar
140g/5oz/scant 1 cup wholemeal flour
100g/3½oz/heaped ¾ cup self-raising flour, plus extra for dusting
1 tsp baking powder
1 tsp ground cinnamon
1 egg, beaten
125ml/4fl oz/½ cup skimmed milk
30g/1oz/¼ cup rolled oats

FOR THE RHUBARB FILLING:
500g/1lb 2oz rhubarb, washed and chopped into 2cm/¾in pieces
4 tbsp agave syrup
1 vanilla pod, split in half lengthways
1 star anise
1 cinnamon stick
2 cardamom pods
grated zest and juice of 1 orange
1 tsp cornflour

Dip two spoons in a little flour, then put spoonfuls of the batter mixture on top of the rhubarb, leaving little gaps in between each spoonful, until you have used all the mixture. Scatter over the oats and bake for 30 minutes until golden brown. Serve hot.

Apple & Plum Crumble

PER SERVING: 6
   FAT 5.6G (OF WHICH SATURATES 3.5G)
   CALORIES 219KCAL
PREPARATION TIME: 20 MINUTES
COOKING TIME: 25 MINUTES

This is a perfect Sunday afternoon pudding after a classic roast. If you have the odd pear, a few blackberries or other bits of fruit that need using up, why not pop them in as well.

Preheat the oven to 180°C/350°F/Gas 4. Put the apples and plums in a bowl and mix with the cinnamon, orange zest and juice. Put the fruit into six 150ml/5fl oz/scant ⅔ cup ramekins.

Mix together the sugar and flour in a bowl and rub in the butter until the mixture resembles breadcrumbs. Finally drizzle over the agave syrup and stir in. Scatter the crumble mixture over the fruit.

Bake for 25 minutes until the apples are tender and the top is golden brown. Serve hot.

Makes 6 crumbles (6 servings)

500g/1lb 2oz eating apples, peeled, cored and cut into 1 cm/½in chunks
4 plums, pitted and cut into 1 cm/½in chunks
1 tsp ground cinnamon
grated zest and juice of 1 orange
2 tbsp caster sugar
110g/3¾oz/scant 1 cup self-raising flour
40g/1½oz butter
2 tbsp agave syrup

  3 months assembled but uncooked

Meringues & Other Bakes

Clouds are fat- and calorie-free but don't taste nearly as good

That's true – and they are more difficult to make! For many years, meringues were my most feared baked food, which is never a good thing when you are known for your baking.

When I was a junior working behind the scenes of a TV show in the prep kitchen, fear would pass over me when I saw the word 'meringue' on the call sheet. If I was in a bad mood or just really tired after an early alarm for work, my meringue mixture would always look like soup rather than light, fluffy clouds. It was as if they could judge my mood.

After a particularly bad day in the kitchen when I had made four batches of soup-like mixture for a Michelin-starred chef, I arrived home at 10pm and made batch after batch of meringues and cooked until 2am. I just needed to get over it – and I did. I can now quite happily make meringues, whether I am in a good or bad mood, but I do smile every time they turn out right.

Meringue Nests with Rose Cream & Fresh Berries

PER SERVING:
   FAT 1.2G (OF WHICH SATURATES 0.8G)
   CALORIES 124KCAL
PREPARATION TIME: 15 MINUTES
COOKING TIME: 2 HOURS

I always know when my mum is on a low-fat diet because there are meringues in the cupboard – they are the perfect, low-fat treat when a sweet craving hits. I've given the classic combination a light, healthy makeover by substituting yogurt and crème fraîche for the usual cream. The slightly sour taste of the yogurt is balanced by the sweetness of the honey and meringue, and the low-fat crème fraîche adds a touch of creaminess, so there are no sacrifices of taste with this low-fat dish.

Preheat the oven to 110°C/225°F/Gas ½. Cut two sheets of baking paper to fit two baking trays. Draw 6 x 8cm/3¼in circles in pencil on the paper.

In a clean bowl, whisk the egg whites, using an electric mixer, until stiff peaks form. Gradually add half the sugar and continue whisking until thick and glossy, then use a large metal spoon to gently fold in the rest of the sugar. Put the meringue mixture into a piping bag fitted with a large star nozzle. Dab a little of the mixture on the corners of the prepared baking tray to hold the baking paper in place, then put the paper on the baking trays so the pencil is underneath but visible through the paper. Pipe the meringue mixture into 6 little nests, using the circles as a guide. Start with a 'blob' in the centre, pipe a spiral around it, then pipe a circle on the outside edge to create a raised border. Repeat with the remaining mixture to make 6 meringues in total.

Bake the meringue nests for 2 hours until dry, then transfer to a wire rack to cool.

Mix together the yogurt, crème fraîche, honey and rose water, then spoon some into the centre of each nest. Top with the berries to serve.

Makes 6 meringues (6 servings)

4 egg whites
180g/6¼oz/heaped ¾ cup caster sugar
170g/6oz/⅔ cup fat-free natural Greek yogurt
3 tbsp low-fat crème fraîche
1 tbsp clear honey
a few drops of rose water or vanilla extract
2 handfuls of mixed berries, such as raspberries, blueberries and sliced strawberries

 7 days before assembling

Mulled Wine Pavlova

PER SERVING:
  FAT 0G
  CALORIES 228KCAL
PREPARATION TIME: 30 MINUTES
COOKING TIME: 1½ HOURS

This makes a great centrepiece pudding at any time of year but it works especially perfectly for Christmas. The deep colour of the poached fruits and their spiced aroma makes the house smell like Christmas and it's a great pudding for sharing.

Preheat the oven to 150°C/300°F/Gas 2 and cut a sheet of baking paper to fit a baking tray. Draw a 23cm/9in circle on the paper, then put it on the tray so the pencil is underneath but still visible.

In a clean bowl, whisk the egg whites, using an electric mixer, until stiff peaks form. Gradually add the caster sugar and continue whisking until thick and glossy. Gently fold in the cornflour and wine vinegar. Use the circle as a guide to gradually spoon the mixture onto the baking paper, starting with the outside, then spooning the remaining meringue into the centre to create a crater. Bake for 1½ hours, then turn the oven off and leave the pavlova in the oven until completely cold.

Mix together the agave syrup and yogurt. Scrape the seeds from the vanilla pod into the yogurt, stir, cover and chill in the fridge. Reserve the vanilla pod.

While the meringue is cooking and cooling, put the wine, orange juice, brown sugar, reserved vanilla pod, spices and orange zest in a saucepan over a medium heat and bring to the boil. Add the pears, reduce the heat to low and simmer gently for about 5 minutes, or until the pears are starting to soften, then add the plums and simmer for a further minute. Remove the pan from the heat and leave to cool. Transfer 4 tablespoons of the poaching liquid to a small saucepan and bring to the boil, then simmer until reduced to a thick syrup. Leave to cool.

Makes a 23cm/9in meringue (12 servings)

FOR THE MERINGUE:
4 egg whites
200g/7oz/heaped ¾ cup caster sugar
1 tsp cornflour
1 tsp white wine vinegar

FOR THE YOGURT FILLING:
1 tbsp agave syrup
200g/7oz/heaped ¾ cup thick, fat-free natural yogurt
1 vanilla pod, split in half lengthways

FOR THE FRUIT TOPPING:
200ml/7fl oz/scant 1 cup red wine
200ml/7fl oz/scant 1 cup orange juice
50g/1¾oz/heaped ¼ cup dark soft brown sugar
1 cinnamon stick
1 star anise
5 black peppercorns
grated zest of 1 orange
4 pears, peeled, with stalks left on
4 plums, halved and pitted
4 figs, halved

 5 days before assembling

When ready to serve, spoon the yogurt into the centre of the pavlova. Remove the fruit from the liquid using a slotted spoon (I freeze the remaining liquid for the next time) and drain well. Cut the cores out of the pears from underneath so they remain whole. Pile the pears, plums and figs on the centre of the pavlova. Finally drizzle over the reduced poaching liquid and serve.

Mango & Basil Meringue Roulade

PER SERVING:
FAT 1.3G (OF WHICH SATURATES 1.6G)
CALORIES 105KCAL
PREPARATION TIME: 30 MINUTES
COOKING TIME: 15 MINUTES

Mango, lime and basil are a classic flavour combination in Thai cooking, albeit Thai basil. The sweetness of the mango is cut perfectly by the lime, while its perfumed flavour is brought out by the basil. Basil has a tendency to go dark when it gets wet or is cut so roll everything up at the last minute so the dessert looks its best.

Preheat the oven to 180°C/350°F/Gas 4 and line a 23 x 30cm/9 x 12in Swiss roll tin with baking paper.

In a clean bowl, whisk the egg whites, using an electric mixer, until stiff peaks form. You should be able to turn the bowl upside down and the whites should not fall out. Gradually add the caster sugar and continue whisking until thick and glossy. Spoon the mixture into the prepared Swiss roll tin and spread it evenly. Bake for 15 minutes until crisp and lightly golden. Leave to cool completely in the tray.

While the meringue is cooling, peel the mangoes. Cut the cheeks from both mangoes by cutting straight down each side of the fruit, and leave to one side. Remove any remaining flesh from the pit and put it in a small food processor along with one cheek and blend to a purée. Cut the remaining mango into thin slices.

Mix together half the mango purée and all the crème fraîche, the lime zest and a squeeze of the juice. Reserve the remaining purée for later. Gather the basil leaves together and shred with a knife. Stir these into the crème fraîche and mango mixture.

Put a large piece of baking paper on a work surface and quickly invert the meringue in its tin onto the paper. Remove the tin and carefully peel back the

Makes a 29cm/11½in roulade (12 servings)

4 egg whites
200g/7oz/heaped ¾ cup caster sugar
2 large ripe mangos
3 tbsp low-fat crème fraîche
grated zest and juice of 1 lime
10 basil leaves
1 tbsp icing sugar, sifted (optional)
1 basil sprig (optional)

baking paper from the base. Turn it so that the short end is nearest you. Spoon the mango purée and crème fraîche mixture onto the meringue and spread it evenly, leaving a 1cm/½in border clear at the far end. Put the mango slices horizontally on top of the purée. Using the baking paper to help, roll the meringue up, starting at the short edge nearest to you and continuing to roll everything up until you get to the end, making sure you finish with the edge underneath.

Dust lightly with icing sugar, if you like, then cut into 12 slices and serve with the remaining mango purée and a sprig of basil, if you like.

Apple & Ginger Strudel

PER SERVING:
 FAT 1.3G (OF WHICH SATURATES 0.5G)
 CALORIES 213KCAL
PREPARATION TIME: 35 MINUTES
COOKING TIME: 30 MINUTES

Apple strudel is a delicious, fruity and naturally light dessert – but you can easily end up with a soggy bottom. But in this recipe, the breadcrumbs help soak up any juices so there's a much better chance of a crispy one. If only getting rid of a saggy bottom was that simple!

Preheat the oven to 190°C/375°F/Gas 5 and line two baking trays with baking paper. Mix together the apples, orange zest and juice, stem ginger, ground ginger, raisins and cornflour.

Unroll the pastry sheets and put one on the baking tray, keeping the sheets you are not using covered in a damp tea towel to prevent them from drying out. Spray with a little low-calorie cooking oil spray, then put the next one on top, spray again, then repeat with one more sheet. Then do the same process on the other tray, making 2 strudels with 3 sheets of pastry each. Do not spray the top sheets of pastry with oil but instead sprinkle over the breadcrumbs, leaving a 2cm/¾in border all the way round.

Divide the apple mixture between the 2 top sheets of pastry, keeping the border around the edges. Roll the pastry up lengthways, tucking in everything as you go so that you have a long cylinder with the seal on the bottom. Spray with a little more oil, then bake for 30 minutes until golden. Cut into portions and serve the strudel hot or cold.

Makes 2 strudels (6 servings)

600g/1lb 5oz eating apples, peeled, cored and cut into 1cm/½in chunks
grated zest of 1 orange
juice of ½ orange
6 balls of stem ginger, finely diced
1 tsp ground ginger
50g/1¾oz/heaped ⅓ cup raisins
1 tsp cornflour
6 sheets of filo pastry, 34 x 30cm/13½ x 12in each
low-calorie cooking oil spray
4 tbsp dried breadcrumbs

  3 months

Swiss Roll

PER SERVING:
    FAT 2.8G (OF WHICH SATURATES 1G)
    CALORIES 196KCAL
PREPARATION TIME: 30 MINUTES
COOKING TIME: 15 MINUTES

This is a case of 'pimp' my Swiss roll. Shop-bought Swiss rolls are usually an ultra sweet sponge, filled with vast amounts of super sweet, cheap jam that has probably never seen a strawberry in its life. This, on the other hand, is filled with fresh fruit and served with a berry compôte, making it perfect for an afternoon treat or super pudding.

Preheat the oven to 200°C/400°F/Gas 6 and line a 30 x 23cm/12 x 9in Swiss roll tin with baking paper.

Put the eggs and sugar in a large bowl and whisk, using an electric mixer, for about 5 minutes until light and creamy. Use a large metal spoon to fold in the flour, taking care not to overmix at this stage. Spoon the mixture into the prepared tin and bake for 7–10 minutes, or until lightly golden and springy to the touch.

Put a large piece of baking paper on a flat surface. Carefully turn the sponge out onto the paper and peel away the baking paper lining, then cover with a clean tea towel and leave to cool.

Meanwhile, put the frozen mixed berries and agave syrup in a saucepan over a medium heat. Scrape the seeds from the vanilla pod into the syrup, then add the vanilla pod and bring to a simmer. Turn the heat down to low and simmer gently for about 5 minutes until the berries start to release their juices. Simmer for a further 5 minutes until slightly thickened. Leave to cool until ready to use, removing the vanilla pod.

When the sponge is cold, spread over the yogurt and scatter over the berries. Turn the sponge so

Makes a 30cm/12in roll (6 servings)

3 eggs
75g/2½oz/⅓ cup caster sugar
75g/2½oz/scant ⅔ cup self-raising flour
250g/9oz/2 cups frozen mixed berries
3 tbsp agave syrup
1 vanilla pod, split in half lengthways
100g/3½oz/scant ½ cup low-fat strawberry
    or raspberry yogurt, as natural as possible,
    flavoured and sweetened with fruit
200g/7oz/1⅔ cups mixed berries, large ones
    like strawberries cut in quarters

that the short edge is nearest you. Cut off a 1cm/½in strip from the edge nearest to you, but leave it in the same place to give you a pivot point to roll the sponge around. Use the baking paper to help you roll the sponge up, making sure you finish with the seal on the bottom. Cut the Swiss roll into 6 slices and serve with the berry sauce.

Passion Fruit Mille-Feuille

PER SERVING:
    FAT 4.2G (OF WHICH SATURATES 2.5G)
    CALORIES 107KCAL
PREPARATION TIME: 35 MINUTES
COOKING TIME: 16 MINUTES

Mille-feuille literally translates as 'a thousand leaves', which are represented by the layers of puff pastry in the traditional version. However, for those of us wanting to watch the fat and calories, a thousand leaves is a little excessive so I have adapted the recipe to use filo pastry. You still get thin layers of crispy pastry with a creamy filling between but with far fewer calories and less fat. It makes a great summer dessert.

Preheat the oven to 180°C/350°F/Gas 4 and spray a non-stick baking tray with a little low-calorie cooking oil spray.

Take 2 sheets of filo pastry and lightly brush with a little of the melted butter. Put another sheet of pastry on each one, then brush lightly with butter again. Cut each of the piles of pastry into 3 long strips, then cut each strip across into 6, so you end up with 36 squares of pastry. Cover the prepared baking tray with pastry squares and put another baking tray on top. Bake the pastry between the baking trays (this will stop them from rising) for 6–8 minutes until golden brown. Repeat with the remaining pastry, then leave to cool.

Mix together the ricotta, 2 tablespoons of the icing sugar, the custard and lemon curd. Spoon into a piping bag fitted with a 1cm/½in plain nozzle.

To assemble the mille-feuille, put 12 pastry squares on a board, then pipe a border around the edge of each one with half the filling mixture. Spoon over half the passion fruit seeds, then top each one with another pastry square. Pipe on the remaining filling mix, then scatter with the remaining passion fruit seeds, then top with pastry. Dust with icing sugar and serve within an hour or so of assembling.

Makes 12 squares (12 servings)

low-calorie cooking oil spray, for greasing
4 sheets of filo pastry, 34 x 30cm/13½ x 12in each
30g/1oz butter, melted
250g/9oz ricotta cheese
3 tbsp icing sugar, sifted
150g/5½oz/scant ⅔ cup Guilt-Free Vanilla Custard (see page 19)
3 tbsp lemon curd
4 passion fruit, halved and seeds scooped out

Banana & Strawberry Soufflés

PER SERVING:
FAT 2.5G (OF WHICH SATURATES 1.3G)
CALORIES 166KCAL
PREPARATION TIME: 20 MINUTES
COOKING TIME: 15 MINUTES

I have a confession to make. Although this recipe is entirely my own, I got the idea from a great chef friend and colleague of mine, Mr Gino D'Acampo. It's so simple as there is no custard or roux base to make first but instead it uses puréed bananas. So simple yet effective.

Preheat the oven to 200°C/400°F/Gas 6. Brush the insides of six 150ml/5fl oz/scant ⅔ cup ramekins with melted butter, then dust with 1 tablespoon of the sugar. Put the ripe bananas in a blender with the strawberries and blend until smooth.

In a clean bowl, whisk the egg whites, using an electric mixer, until stiff peaks form. Gradually add the remaining sugar and continue whisking until thick and glossy. Carefully and gradually, fold the egg whites into the banana and strawberry mixture.

Spoon the mixture into the prepared ramekins, levelling the tops with the back of a knife. Run your thumb around the edge of the ramekins so that they are clean, then pop them on a tray and bake for 12–15 minutes until risen.

Meanwhile, make the sauce. Put the strawberries and sugar in a small saucepan over a low heat. Scrape the seeds from the vanilla pod into the mixture, then add the vanilla pod. Heat for a few minutes until the strawberries are softened, warmed through and releasing their juices. Remove from the heat, remove the vanilla pod and serve the sauce with the hot soufflés.

Makes 6 soufflés (6 servings)

FOR THE BANANA SOUFFLÉS:
15g/½oz butter, melted
50g/1¾oz/scant ¼ cup caster sugar, plus 1 tbsp for dusting
3 ripe bananas
150g/5½oz/1 cup strawberries, hulled
6 egg whites

FOR THE STRAWBERRY SAUCE:
650g/1lb 7oz/4⅓ cups strawberries, hulled and halved
1 tbsp caster sugar
1 vanilla pod, split in half lengthways

Raspberry & Chocolate Choux Buns

PER SERVING:
  FAT 2G (OF WHICH SATURATES 0G)
  CALORIES 130KCAL
PREPARATION TIME: 25 MINUTES, PLUS
  30 MINUTES COOLING
COOKING TIME: 40 MINUTES

For those of you who like profiteroles, this is for you. Instead of being filled with whipped cream, these are packed with fresh raspberries and a low-fat chocolate pastry cream. If you want to make the buns in advance, do not fill them but store the hollow buns in an airtight container for a few days.

Preheat the oven to 200°C/400°F/Gas 6 and line two baking trays with baking paper.

To make the choux pastry, put the butter and sugar in a saucepan with 150ml/5fl oz/scant ⅔ cup water and bring to the boil over a medium heat. Tip in the flour and beat with a wooden spoon for 1 minute until the mixture is smooth and and comes away from the sides of the pan to form a ball. Take the pan off the heat and gradually beat in enough of the eggs, one at a time, until the mixture is soft enough to drop off the spoon in lumps.

Put 24 teaspoonfuls of the mixture on the prepared baking trays, leaving a 4cm/1½in gap between each one. Run your hands under the tap, then flick them over the buns to dampen them. Bake for 10 minutes, then turn the oven up to 220°C/425°F/Gas 7 and bake for a further 15 minutes until golden brown.

Use a skewer to make a small hole in the bottom of each bun, then turn them upside down (bottoms up) on a wire rack to cool, allowing steam to escape and prevent them from going soggy.

Meanwhile, make the filling. Put the milk and vanilla extract in a saucepan over a medium heat until lukewarm. In a separate bowl, mix together the eggs, sugar, cocoa powder and cornflour, then

Makes 24 buns (12 servings)

40g/1½oz butter
1 tsp caster sugar
60g/2¼oz/½ cup plain flour
2 eggs, beaten
1 tsp icing sugar, sifted

FOR THE CHOCOLATE & RASPBERRY FILLING:
350ml/12fl oz/scant 1½ cups skimmed milk
1 tsp vanilla extract
2 eggs
2 tbsp caster sugar
1 tbsp cocoa powder, sifted
40g/1½ oz/⅓ cup cornflour
250g/9oz/2 cups raspberries

 2 days
without filling

 1 month
without filling

gradually whisk in the warm milk. Pour the mixture back into a clean saucepan and put over a gentle heat. Stir continuously until it starts to thicken, whisking to get rid of any lumps. Once it starts to bubble, cook for 30 seconds, then remove from the heat and spoon into a bowl. Cover the surface with cling film and leave to cool.

When the choux pastry and pastry cream are both cold, put the pastry cream into a piping bag fitted with a 1.5cm/⅝in plain nozzle. Use a serrated knife to cut open the buns, as though you were opening a bread roll. Pipe the pastry cream onto the bottom half of each bun, top with a few raspberries, then replace the tops and dust with icing sugar to serve.

Coffee Eclairs

PER SERVING:
 FAT 4.6G (OF WHICH SATURATES 2.5G)
 CALORIES 105KCAL
PREPARATION TIME: 25 MINUTES
COOKING TIME: 30 MINUTES

Creamy, soft filling, light, crisp pastry and a splash of icing – the eclair is the perfect combo. I first made these as an ideal all-in-one pudding for a posh picnic – no need for plates or cutlery. The coffee offsets the sweetness to perfection but you could change the filling to vanilla or chocolate, although chocolate will up the calories slightly.

Preheat the oven to 200°C/400°F/Gas 6 and line a baking tray with baking paper.

Put the butter and sugar in a saucepan with 150ml/5fl oz/scant ⅔ cup water and bring to the boil over a medium heat. Turn the heat to low, and beat in the flour with a wooden spoon for 1 minute until the mixture is smooth and comes away from the sides of the pan in a ball. Take off the heat and gradually beat in enough of the eggs until the mixture is soft and will drop off the spoon in lumps.

Spoon the mixture into a piping bag fitted with a 1.5cm/⅝in plain nozzle and pipe 12 long lines 20 x 10cm/8 x 4in on the paper, leaving a 2.5cm/1in gap between each one. Run your hands under the tap, then flick them over the pastry. Bake for 10 minutes, then turn the oven up to 220°C/425°F/Gas 7 and bake for a further 15 minutes until golden brown.

Use a skewer to make a small hole in the bottom of each bun, then turn them upside down (bottoms up) on a wire rack to cool, allowing steam to escape and prevent them from going soggy.

Meanwhile, make the filling. Put the milk and coffee in a saucepan over a low heat and bring to just lukewarm. Mix together the eggs, sugar and cornflour, then gradually whisk in the milk. Pour

Makes 12 eclairs (12 servings)

FOR THE ECLAIRS:
40g/1½oz butter
1 tsp caster sugar
80g/2¾oz/scant ⅔ cup plain flour
2 eggs, beaten

FOR THE COFFEE FILLING:
350ml/12fl oz/scant 1½ cups skimmed milk
1 tbsp instant coffee granules
2 eggs
2 tbsp caster sugar
40g/1½oz/⅓ cup cornflour

FOR THE CHOCOLATE TOPPING:
50g/1¾oz dark chocolate, 70% cocoa solids

  1 month without filling

the mixture back into a clean saucepan over a low heat, whisking continuously until the mixture starts to bubble and thicken. Cook for 30 seconds, then remove from the heat and spoon into a bowl. Cover the surface with cling film and leave to cool.

Put the pastry cream into a piping bag fitted with a plain 1.5cm/⅝in nozzle. Use a serrated knife to slice the eclairs in half. Pipe a line of cream down the centre of each one and replace the top. Put the chocolate in a large heatproof bowl and rest it over a saucepan of gently simmering water, making sure the bottom of the bowl does not touch the water. Heat, stirring, until the chocolate has melted. Drizzle over the eclairs and leave to set before serving.

Whoopeeeeeeeeee Pies

PER SERVING:
FAT 1.3G (OF WHICH SATURATES 0.7G)
CALORIES 115KCAL
PREPARATION TIME: 25 MINUTES
COOKING TIME: 10 MINUTES

I know this is an overly excessive use of e in a recipe title but the fact that these are low fat makes people go 'whoopeeeeeeeee' rather than just 'whoopee'!

Preheat the oven to 170°C/325°F/Gas 3 and line two baking trays with baking paper.

Beat together the sugar and bananas in a bowl until well blended. Mix in the eggs and milk. In a separate bowl, mix together the flour, cocoa powder, baking powder, cream of tartar and salt. Add the wet ingredients to the dry ingredients and mix together well to form a thick batter.

Put the batter into a piping bag fitted with a 1.5cm/⅝in plain nozzle and pipe 48 rounds on the prepared baking trays. Alternatively, you can do this by spooning the mixture on with two teaspoons. Bake for 8–10 minutes, or until a skewer inserted in the centre comes out clean. Leave to cool in the tin for 5 minutes, then lift off the paper and transfer to a wire rack.

Meanwhile, put the marshmallows in a non-stick saucepan over a low heat and gently warm until melted. Put 1 teaspoon melted marshmallow in the centre of a pie, then top with another and press down lightly. Repeat with the remaining pies and melted marshmallows. Serve warm or leave to cool.

Makes 24 pies (12 servings)

FOR THE WHOOPEE PIES:
150g/5½oz/⅔ cup caster sugar
2 large ripe bananas, lightly mashed
2 eggs, beaten
230ml/7¾fl oz/scant 1 cup skimmed milk
250g/9oz/2 cups plain flour
125g/4½oz/heaped 1⅓ cups cocoa powder, sifted
1½ tsp baking powder
½ tsp cream of tartar
a pinch of fine sea salt

FOR THE MARSHMALLOW FILLING:
100g/3½oz marshmallows

 3 days ❄ 3 months without filling

Macaroons

PER SERVING:
  FAT 4G (OF WHICH SATURATES 0.2G)
  CALORIES 200KCAL
PREPARATION TIME: 30 MINUTES, PLUS
  15 MINUTES STANDING
COOKING TIME: 15 MINUTES

Macaroons are perennially popular but be warned – despite being small and light, the buttery, creamy filling can bump up the calories. It's a real case of looks being deceptive. My version is lighter than a normal macaroon as I have reduced the quantity of ground almonds and given them a much lighter filling. They can be tricky to make but once you have mastered this skill, you can get inventive with flavours and colours and they never fail to impress. These are best eaten within a couple of days so store them in an airtight container in the fridge or just tuck in!

Preheat the oven to 160°C/315°F/Gas 2½ and line two baking trays with baking paper.

Put the ground almonds and icing sugar in a food processor and blend until really fine. In a clean bowl, whisk the egg whites, using an electric mixer, until stiff peaks form. Gradually add the caster sugar and continue whisking until thick and glossy. Carefully fold in the almond and icing sugar mixture, using a metal spoon.

Carefully fold in a little pink food colouring and a few drops of almond extract, if you like. Put the mixture into a piping bag fitted with a 1cm/½in round nozzle. Pipe 48 circles of about 2.5cm/1in in diameter onto the baking trays. Give the trays a sharp tap on the work surface, then leave at room temperature for 10–15 minutes, or until a skin has formed on the surface. Once you can lightly touch the macaroons with your finger and the mixture does not stick to you, they are ready to cook. Bake them in the oven for 15 minutes until golden and crisp with a dry top. Transfer to a wire rack to cool.

Makes 24 macaroons (12 servings)

FOR THE MARACOONS:
100g/3½oz/1 cup ground almonds
175g/6oz/scant 1½ cups icing sugar, sifted
3 egg whites
75g/2½oz/⅓ cup caster sugar
a few drops of pink food colouring (optional)
a few drops of almond extract (optional)

FOR THE WHITE CHOCOLATE FILLING:
75g/2½oz white chocolate, diced
100ml/3½fl oz/scant ½ cup buttermilk
75g/2½oz/scant ⅔ cup icing sugar, sifted

 3 days

To make the filling, put the chocolate in a large heatproof bowl and rest it over a saucepan of gently simmering water, making sure the bottom of the bowl does not touch the water. Once the chocolate starts to melt, turn the heat off and let the residual heat melt the rest – this will prevent the chocolate from splitting, which white chocolate is particularly prone to do. Once the chocolate has melted, gently fold in the buttermilk, then sift over and stir in the icing sugar. (At this stage you can flavour the filling with peppermint or vanilla extract, if you wish.) Leave this mixture to cool and firm up.

Once the macaroons and filling are cool, put the filling in a piping bag with a 1cm/½in plain nozzle. Pipe a little in the centre of half of the macaroons and then top with the other half and enjoy.

Sultana Pinwheels

PER SERVING:
FAT 3.5G (OF WHICH SATURATES 1.2G)
CALORIES 285KCAL
PREPARATION TIME: 20 MINUTES, PLUS 3 HOURS
RISING
COOKING TIME: 20 MINUTES

My mum loves a *pain au raisin* with a coffee when she's treating herself, but they are so high in fat from all the butter in the croissant dough that even on a treat day, they seem a little excessive. This is my take on that classic French pastry, replacing croissant dough with traditional bread dough, which is much lighter in calories and fat.

Mix together the flour, salt, caster sugar, mixed spice and yeast in a bowl, then make a well in the centre. Gradually add the beaten egg followed by the milk and mix everything together to make a soft dough.

Turn the dough out onto a lightly floured surface and knead for 10 minutes, or until the dough is smooth and elastic. Lightly oil a large bowl with low-calorie cooking oil spray. Put the dough in the bowl, cover with cling film and leave in a warm place for 2 hours, or until doubled in size.

Line a baking tray with baking paper. Turn the dough out onto a lightly floured work surface and knock the air out of the dough by punching it with your fist. Use your fingers to press the dough down, then take a rolling pin to roll it into a large rectangle 20 x 30 x 1cm/8 x 12 x ½in. Spread the butter over the surface, then sprinkle over the brown sugar, sultanas and cinnamon. Roll up tightly, starting at the long edge and tucking everything in as you go, finishing with the join on top. Pinch the edges together to prevent it from unravelling, then roll it so the join is on the bottom.

Use a sharp knife to cut the long sausage into 12 pinwheels. Put the pinwheels on their sides on the baking tray (so you can see the swirly side

Makes 12 pinwheels (12 servings)

550g/1lb 4oz/4⅓ cups strong white flour,
  plus extra for dusting
1 tsp fine sea salt
3½ tbsp caster sugar
2 tsp mixed spice
7g/¼oz/2 tsp fast-action dried yeast
1 egg, beaten
275ml/9¾fl oz/generous 1 cup skimmed milk
low-calorie cooking oil spray, for greasing
45g/1½oz butter, softened
2 tbsp light soft brown sugar
125g/4½oz/1 cup sultanas
1 tsp ground cinnamon
55g/2oz/scant ½ cup icing sugar, sifted

 1 day 2 months

facing upwards). Cover with a piece of greased baking paper, then leave to rise for a further hour, or until doubled in size.

Preheat the oven to 200°C/400°F/Gas 6. Remove the covering paper and bake the pinwheels for 15–20 minutes until golden brown, then transfer to a wire rack to cool.

Meanwhile, put the icing sugar in a bowl and add about 2 tablespoons water, a teaspoonful at a time, until you have a thick paste that slowly runs off a spoon. Drizzle the icing over the pinwheels, then leave to set for 5 minutes before tucking into a delicious pinwheel.

Chocolate, Rum & Raisin Samosas

PER SERVING:
    FAT 6G (OF WHICH SATURATES 3.3G)
    CALORIES 256KCAL
PREPARATION TIME: 30 MINUTES, PLUS
    20 MINUTES SOAKING
COOKING TIME: 10 MINUTES

We tend to think of samosas as savoury starters but in India they also make sweet versions, which inspired me to make these. If you have difficulty folding them into the triangle shapes, you can always just roll them into spring roll shapes instead – just make sure you tuck in the ends.

Put the raisins in a bowl with the rum and leave to soak for 20 minutes. Preheat the oven to 190°C/375°F/Gas 5 and line a baking tray with baking paper.

Put the chocolate in a large heatproof bowl and rest it over a saucepan of gently simmering water, making sure the bottom of the bowl does not touch the water. Heat, stirring occasionally, until the chocolate has melted. Remove from the heat and stir in the soaked raisins.

Take 1 strip of pastry, keeping the rest of the strips covered in a damp tea towel to prevent them from drying out, and put 1 teaspoon of the chocolate mixture at one end. Take one corner next to the chocolate and fold it over, creating a triangle and covering the chocolate mix. Keep folding the pastry over, encasing all the filling, to create a triangular-shaped parcel, stopping before you make the final fold. Brush the end of the pastry with a little melted butter, then fold and press the edges to seal. Put it, seal-side down, on the prepared baking tray. Brush the top with butter and repeat with the remaining pastry and filling.

Bake for 5–10 minutes until golden brown. Dust with icing sugar and serve with a scoop of frozen yogurt, if you like.

Makes 12 samosas (12 servings)

200g/7oz/scant 1⅔ cups raisins
2 tbsp dark rum
100g/3½oz dark chocolate, 70% cocoa solids
4 sheets of filo pastry, 34 x 30cm/13½ x 12in each, cut lengthways into 3 long thin strips
30g/1oz butter, melted
½ tsp icing sugar, sifted, for dusting
12 small scoops of Guilt-Free Frozen Vanilla Yogurt (see page 21), to serve (optional)

Cranberry & Cinnamon Hot Cross Buns

PER SERVING:
FAT 4.2G (OF WHICH SATURATES 1.3G)
CALORIES 276KCAL
PREPARATION TIME: 30 MINUTES, PLUS 2 HOURS
40 MINUTES RISING
COOKING TIME: 15 MINUTES

Traditionally, hot cross buns are eaten during the Christian celebration of Lent, either warm or toasted, but I think these are far too good just to eat once a year. I love the high shine you get on the top, which is achieved by brushing warm syrup over the hot, baked buns. Of course, you could leave off the cross if that doesn't seem right in July.

Mix together the strong flour and cinnamon in a bowl, then rub in the butter, using your fingertips, until the mixture resembles coarse breadcrumbs. Stir in the sugar, orange zest and yeast. Make a well in the centre of the flour and add the beaten egg, followed by the milk. Bring everything together to make a soft dough.

Turn the dough out onto a lightly floured surface and sprinkle over the cranberries, then knead the dough for 10 minutes until it is elastic and no longer sticky and the cranberries have been incorporated. Lightly spray a clean bowl with low-calorie cooking oil spray, put the dough in the bowl, cover with cling film and leave in a warm place to rise for 2 hours, or until it has doubled in size.

Line two baking trays with baking paper. Knock the air out of the dough by punching it with your fist, then divide it into 12 equal pieces and shape them into balls. Put them on the prepared baking trays, leaving a gap between each one. Cover the buns lightly with a piece of baking paper and leave in a warm place to rise for a further 40 minutes to 1 hour, or until risen.

Preheat the oven to 200°C/400°F/Gas 6.

Makes 12 buns (12 servings)

625g/1lb 6oz/5 cups strong white flour, plus extra for dusting
2 tsp ground cinnamon
40g/1½oz butter
80g/2¾oz/⅓ cup caster sugar
grated zest of 1 orange
7g/¼oz/2 tsp fast-action dried yeast
1 egg, beaten
270ml/9½fl oz/generous 1 cup skimmed milk
70g/2½oz/heaped ½ cup dried cranberries
low-calorie cooking oil spray, for greasing
2 tbsp plain flour
1 tbsp golden syrup

  2 months shaped but uncooked

Mix together the plain flour with a little cold water to make a paste. Spoon into a small piping bag, then pipe a cross on the top of each bun. Bake for 10–15 minutes until golden brown and risen. Transfer to a wire rack to cool slightly.

Warm the golden syrup in a saucepan or the microwave and brush over the tops to give them a nice glaze. Serve warm or toasted.

Scones

PER SERVING:
    FAT 3.2G (OF WHICH SATURATES 2.3G)
    CALORIES 99KCAL
PREPARATION TIME: 15 MINUTES
COOKING TIME: 15 MINUTES

We would always telephone Nanny (my mum's mum) before setting off on the hour-long drive to her house to let her know we were on our way. By the time we arrived, the kitchen would be filled with fruit scones for Mum and Dad, cheese ones for my sister and plain ones for me. They would literally cover every surface. We would all take goody bags home to pop in the freezer. That's why this recipe reminds me of Nanny and her amazing scones.

Preheat the oven to 200°C/400°F/Gas 6 and lightly flour a non-stick baking tray.

Put the flour in a large bowl, then rub in the butter, using your fingertips, until the mixture resembles breadcrumbs. Stir in the sugar, then use a fork to gradually mix in the milk and blend to a soft dough.

Turn the dough out onto a lightly floured surface and knead very lightly until smooth. (Kneading it too much will develop the gluten in the flour and make the scones tough – more like rock cakes than scones!) Roll the dough out until it is 2cm/¾in thick, then use a 5cm/2in round pastry cutter to cut out the scones. Gather together any off-cuts and carefully knead once again, as little as possible, then re-roll and cut out any remaining scones.

Put the scones on the prepared baking tray and brush the tops with a little milk. Bake for 12–15 minutes until risen and golden brown.

Transfer to a wire rack to cool. Put a clean tea towel over the cooling scones for 5 minutes, then remove the tea towel and leave to cool completely. This just helps put some steam back into the scones so that they are extra light in the centre.

Makes 12 scones (12 servings)

225g/8oz/heaped 1¾ cups self-raising flour, plus extra for dusting
40g/1½oz butter
30g/1oz/1½ tbsp caster sugar
160ml/5¼fl oz/scant ⅔ cup skimmed milk, plus 1 tbsp, for glazing

 1 day ❄ 3 months

Large Cakes

Love at first bite

Big cakes are the kings and queens of the tea table. They look so impressive placed on beautiful cake stands and plates and are perfect to serve for celebrations with friends and family. They are the cakes for sharing.

Big cakes are often great ones to start making if you are a novice baker, as their size means they look impressive even if they are not iced perfectly. There is also rarely any need for technical piping or precise division of batter between cupcake cases.

One problem you do get with big cakes, which often does not appear in smaller individual ones, is that the cooking time can vary depending on your oven. If you find that the cakes are browning too quickly, before they are cooked through, cover the top of the cake with a piece of kitchen foil until it finishes cooking. Next time, reduce your oven temperature by 10°C/50°F/one Gas mark and you should be fine.

Happy baking and very happy celebrating.

Apple & Cinnamon Crumble Cake

PER SERVING:
    FAT 3.4G (OF WHICH SATURATES 1.5G)
    CALORIES 182KCAL
PREPARATION TIME: 15 MINUTES
COOKING TIME: 1 HOUR

When a combination works as well as apple and cinnamon, why only use it in traditional crumble? This recipe covers the best of both worlds: a delicious cake made with low-fat yogurt combines with chunks of apple, keeping it moist in the centre, and complemented by a crumbly cinnamon topping for a bit of extra crunch. It's also great toasted.

Preheat the oven to 180°C/350°F/Gas 4. Grease a 900g/2lb loaf tin with low-calorie cooking oil spray.

Beat together the eggs, caster sugar, yogurt and vanilla extract, using an electric mixer, until light and creamy. Sift over the self-raising flour, 1 teaspoon of the cinnamon and the baking powder and fold in, then stir in the grated and diced apple. Spoon the mixture into the prepared loaf tin.

Put the plain flour in a large bowl, then rub in the butter, using your fingertips, until the mixture resembles fine breadcrumbs. Stir in the granulated sugar and the remaining cinnamon, then sprinkle the mixture over the top of the cake. Bake for 1 hour until the top is golden brown, or until a skewer inserted in the centre comes out clean.

Leave to cool in the tin for 10 minutes, then carefully transfer to a wire rack to cool completely.

Makes a 900g/2lb loaf (12 servings)

low-calorie cooking oil spray, for greasing
3 eggs
125g/4½oz/heaped ½ cup caster sugar
200g/7oz/heaped ¾ cup fat-free natural yogurt
1 tsp vanilla extract
225g/8oz/heaped 1¾ cups self-raising flour
2 tsp ground cinnamon
2 tsp baking powder
3 apples, cored, skin on, 2 grated and 1 chopped into 1cm/½in dice
40g/1½oz/⅓ cup plain flour
30g/1oz butter
30g/1oz/2 tbsp granulated sugar

 2 days   3 months

Austrian-Style Rhubarb Cake

PER SERVING:
    FAT 4.4G (OF WHICH SATURATES 0.2G)
    CALORIES 154KCAL
PREPARATION TIME: 15 MINUTES PLUS
    30 MINUTES MARINATING
COOKING TIME: 40 MINUTES

My dear school friend Heidi's mother is from Austria and can I can remember going round to her house and being fed cakes and bakes that tasted like no British bake I had ever eaten. I was absolutely fascinated by them all but three stood out for me – Christmas biscuits, apricot dumplings and this rhubarb cake. This is my adaptation of her cake, just a little lighter.

Preheat the oven to 180°C/350°F/Gas 4. Grease a 23cm/9in loose-based cake tin with low-calorie spray oil and line the base with baking paper.

Put the chunks of rhubarb in a bowl and sprinkle over 2 tablespoons of the sugar. Leave for 30 minutes, then drain off all the water and pat it dry. Dust with cornflour and toss together.

Beat together the butter and sugar, using an electric mixer, until light and creamy. Beat in the eggs, one at a time, then fold in the flour and baking powder.

Spoon the batter into the prepared cake tin and smooth the top with a spatula. Top this with the dried rhubarb and bake for 40 minutes until a skewer inserted in the centre comes out clean.

Leave to cool in the tin for 15 minutes, then transfer to a wire rack to cool completely.

Makes a 23cm/9in cake (12 servings)

low-calorie cooking oil spray, for greasing
500g/1lb 2oz rhubarb, trimmed and cubed
125g/4½oz/heaped ½ cup caster sugar
1 tbsp cornflour
50g/1¾oz butter, softened
2 eggs
175g/6oz/heaped 1⅓ cups plain flour
2 tsp baking powder

Raspberry, Pear & Oat Loaf

PER SERVING:
  FAT 5G (OF WHICH SATURATES 2.5G)
  CALORIES 177KCAL
PREPARATION TIME: 15 MINUTES, PLUS
  15 MINUTES SOAKING
COOKING TIME: 1 HOUR

I believe oats are a super food – they soak up cholesterol in your blood, helping to reduce it naturally. I designed this cake for my dad, who has high cholesterol despite following a healthy lifestyle. This is a treat for him as it combines his favourite fruit, pears, with oats that hold moisture in the cake and make it utterly delicious. Plus it's also almost good for you.

Preheat the oven to 180°C/350°F/Gas 4 and lightly grease a 900g/2lb loaf tin with low-calorie cooking oil spray. Put the oats in a large bowl. Bring the apple juice to the boil in a small saucepan, then pour over the oats and leave to soak for 15 minutes.

Beat together the butter, sugar and vanilla extract, using an electric mixer, until light and creamy. Beat in the eggs one at a time. Fold in the flour and baking powder, then fold the mixture into the soaked oats. Finally, stir in the raspberries and the diced pears.

Spoon the mixture into the prepared loaf tin, sprinkle with remaining oats and bake for 1 hour until golden brown, or until a skewer inserted in the centre comes out clean. Turn out and transfer to a wire rack to cool.

Makes a 900g/2lb loaf (12 servings)

low-calorie cooking oil spray, for greasing
100g/3½oz/1 cup rolled oats, plus 1 tbsp
  for sprinkling
150ml/5fl oz/scant ⅔ cup apple juice
50g/1¾oz butter, softened
75g/2½oz/⅓ cup golden caster sugar
1 tsp vanilla extract
2 eggs
185g/6½oz/1½ cups self-raising flour
1 tsp baking powder
150g/5½oz/1¼ cups raspberries
2 ripe pears, peeled, cored and cut into 1cm/½in dice

 2 days 3 months

Orange, Polenta & Thyme Cake

PER SERVING:
    FAT 6G (OF WHICH SATURATES 1G)
    CALORIES 215KCAL
PREPARATION TIME: 25 MINUTES, PLUS
    20 MINUTES SOAKING
COOKING TIME: 40 MINUTES

This polenta cake has a totally different texture from a normal sponge. There is a slight crunch to it as the polenta holds its texture when cooked. It also absorbs the flavour of the orange as it soaks up the juice and syrup at the end. It's a beautiful summery cake and also makes a modern dessert if served warm with low-fat crème fraîche.

Put the polenta in a bowl, pour over one-third of the orange juice and leave to soak for about 20 minutes, stirring occasionally. Preheat the oven to 170°C/325°F/Gas 3 and line the base of a 23cm/9in non-stick springform cake tin with baking paper.

Meanwhile, grate the zest from the oranges and leave to one side. Cut the top and bottom off both oranges, then use a small knife to carefully cut off the rind and pith, then slice the oranges into 3mm/⅛in rounds. Spread these over the bottom of the cake tin and add the thyme sprigs.

Whisk together the eggs and sugar, using an electric mixer, until light and creamy, then whisk in the oil, the reserved orange zest, the yogurt and thyme leaves. Stir in the soaked polenta.

In a separate bowl, mix together the ground almonds, flour and baking powder. Carefully fold the dry ingredients into the wet ingredients until just combined, then pour the mixture into the prepared cake tin. Bake for 30–40 minutes, or until a skewer inserted in the centre comes out clean.

While the cake is cooking, pour the remaining orange juice into a small saucepan and bring

Makes a 23cm/9in cake (12 servings)

100g/3½oz/⅔ cup fine polenta
300ml/10½fl oz/scant 1¼ cups fresh orange juice
2 oranges
3 thyme sprigs
3 eggs
150g/5½oz/⅔ cup caster sugar
3 tbsp olive oil
100g/3½oz/scant ½ cup fat-free natural yogurt
1 tsp thyme leaves
35g/1¼oz/⅓ cup ground almonds
150g/5½oz/1¼ cups plain flour
1 tsp baking powder

 2 days   ❄ 3 months

to the boil over a high heat. Turn the heat down to low and simmer gently for about 10 minutes until it is thick and syrupy.

Leave to cool completely in the tin, then run a knife around the edge of the tin to release the cake. Put a plate on top of the cake and carefully invert it and remove the tin. Loosen the cake base and peel back the paper. Pour the orange juice syrup over the cake and leave to soak in before serving.

Banana & Rum Cake

PER SERVING:
   FAT 3.5G (OF WHICH SATURATES 0.5G)
   CALORIES 279KCAL
PREPARATION TIME: 15 MINUTES
COOKING TIME: 30 MINUTES, PLUS MAKING THE
   APPLE PURÉE

There are a few things that make my teeth go a little funny when I have to touch them – you know, like fingers scratching down a chalk board. I have learnt to cope with that, but polystyrene and over-ripe bananas still freak me out. However, I also hate wasting food, so I just have to get on with it when it comes to ripe bananas (I find grimacing when peeling helps). This cake is a perfect way to use up bananas that are really ripe and soft and not just because the hint of rum adds an adult twist to the proceedings. It tastes just as good made with honey if you are sharing it with the kids.

Preheat the oven to 180°C/350°F/Gas 4 and lightly grease a 20cm/8in square cake tin with low-calorie cooking oil spray.

Put the eggs, sugar, milk, oil and vanilla extract in a bowl and whisk for 5 minutes, using an electric mixer, until light and creamy, then beat in the apple purée. Mash the very ripe bananas, then beat them into the mixture. Sift in the flour, baking powder, bicarbonate of soda and salt. Fold everything together until blended, then spoon the mixture into the prepared tin.

Cut the ripe banana into very thin slices on the diagonal. Spread the slices on top of the cake, then bake for about 30 minutes until golden brown, or a skewer inserted in the centre comes out clean.

Gently warm the rum and honey in a small saucepan. Remove the cake from the oven and brush the rum mixture over the cake. Leave to cool in the tin for 5 minutes, then transfer to a wire rack to cool completely.

Makes a 20cm/8in square cake (12 servings)

low-calorie cooking oil spray, for greasing
2 eggs
150g/5½oz/⅔ cup caster sugar
5 tbsp skimmed milk
1 tbsp sunflower oil
1 tbsp vanilla extract
4 tbsp Apple Purée (see page 15)
2 very ripe bananas, and 1 ripe banana
225g/8oz/heaped 1¾ cups plain flour
1 tbsp baking powder
1 tsp bicarbonate of soda
½ tsp fine sea salt
2 tbsp rum
2 tsp clear honey

 3 days   3 months

Lemon, Rosemary & Poppy Seed Cake

PER SERVING:
  FAT 5.3G (OF WHICH SATURATES 2.6G)
  CALORIES 250KCAL
PREPARATION TIME: 10 MINUTES, PLUS AT LEAST
  15 MINUTES SOAKING
COOKING TIME: 30 MINUTES

Cakes and herbs may not seem to be natural bedfellows but herbs can make familiar cakes, such as lemon and poppy seed, into totally new creations. Lemon and rosemary work perfectly together in savoury dishes and marinades and now they can lie side by side in sweet treats too.

Put the poppy seeds in a bowl, pour over the warm milk and leave to soak for at least 15 minutes. Preheat the oven to 180°C/350°F/Gas 4 and grease a 25cm/10in fluted ring cake tin (a Bundt tin) with a little low-calorie cooking oil spray.

Beat together the butter and sugar, using an electric mixer, until light and creamy, then add the eggs, flour, soaked poppy seeds, lemon zest, yogurt and chopped rosemary and mix everything together well.

Spoon the mixture into the prepared cake tin and bake for 25–30 minutes, or until a skewer inserted in the centre comes out clean. Leave to cool in the tin for 5 minutes, then transfer to a wire rack to cool completely.

Once the cake has cooled, sift the icing sugar into a small bowl. Whisk in the lemon juice, a few drops at a time, mixing to make a paste. Spoon the icing over the top of the cake. Brush the rosemary sprigs with the beaten egg white, using a pastry brush. Sprinkle over the caster sugar to give the sprigs a frosted effect, then put them on the iced cake to serve.

Makes a 25cm/10in cake (12 servings)

FOR THE LEMON, ROSEMARY & POPPY SEED CAKE:
low-calorie cooking oil spray, for greasing
20g/¾oz poppy seeds
2 tbsp warm skimmed milk
50g/1¾oz butter, softened
200g/7oz/heaped ¾ cup caster sugar
3 eggs
300g/10½oz/heaped 2⅓ cups self-raising flour
grated zest of 2 lemons
100g/3½oz/scant ½ cup fat-free natural yogurt
1 tbsp chopped rosemary leaves

FOR THE LEMON & ROSEMARY TOPPING:
100g/3½oz/heaped ¾ cup icing sugar, sifted
2½ tsp lemon juice
3 rosemary sprigs
1 egg white, lightly beaten
1 tbsp caster sugar

 3 days

Pear, Cocoa & Walnut Upside-Down Cake

PER SERVING:
FAT 5.6G (OF WHICH SATURATES 0.5G)
CALORIES 193KCAL
PREPARATION TIME: 20 MINUTES
COOKING TIME: 40 MINUTES

As a child I was lucky enough to grow up in a house where we had a few fruit trees in the garden. However, they never fruited gradually – all the fruit came at once at the end of September. We had to come up with a variety of recipes other than stewed apples and pears to use up the crop in inventive ways. This upside-down cake was one of my favourites. We always had one or two in the freezer months after the leaves had fallen from the trees. I've made this with fresh pears but you can use a tin of pear halves in natural juice, drained, then you don't need to poach them.

Preheat the oven to 180°C/350°F/Gas 4 and grease the base and sides of a 23cm/9in cake tin with low-calorie cooking oil spray.

Put the pears in a saucepan with 500ml/17fl oz/ 2 cups water and the caster sugar over a medium heat. Bring to the boil, then turn the heat down to low and simmer for 5 minutes until just tender when pierced with the tip of a knife. Remove from the heat, drain and leave to cool slightly.

Arrange two-thirds of the pear pieces in the bottom of the prepared cake tin, then scatter with the walnut halves. Mix together the brown sugar and cocoa powder, then sprinkle over the pears. Purée the remaining pear halves and measure out 150g/5½oz of the purée.

To make the topping, mix together the flour, baking powder, cinnamon and cocoa powder in a large bowl. In a separate bowl, whisk together the sugar, eggs, pear purée and oil until blended. Add the wet ingredients to the dry ingredients and mix until just combined. Pour the cake batter over the pears in

Makes a 23cm/9in cake (12 servings)

FOR THE WALNUT & CHOCOLATE BASE:
low-calorie cooking oil spray, for greasing
4 pears, peeled, cored and halved or quartered
100g/3½oz/scant ½ cup caster sugar
12 walnut halves
1 tbsp light soft brown sugar
1 tbsp cocoa powder, sifted

FOR THE CHOCOLATE TOPPING:
150g/5½oz/1¼ cups self-raising flour
2 tsp baking powder
2 tsp ground cinnamon
6 tbsp cocoa powder, sifted
150g/5½oz/heaped ¾ cup light soft brown sugar
2 eggs
3 tbsp sunflower oil
½ tsp icing sugar, sifted, for dusting

 2 days   3 months

the bottom of the prepared tin and bake for about 30 minutes, or until a skewer inserted in the centre comes out clean. Turn the cake out upside down onto a serving plate, dust with icing sugar and serve warm, or leave to cool.

Summer Berry Gateau

PER SERVING:
FAT 5G (OF WHICH SATURATES 2G)
CALORIES 219KCAL
PREPARATION TIME: 20 MINUTES, PLUS
20 MINUTES WHISKING
COOKING TIME: 35 MINUTES

The word gateau conjures up images of decadent cakes filled with whipped cream and berries, and although they look beautiful, I think they can be a little bit sickly sweet and heavy. This sponge, on the other hand, is a classic Genoise sponge made with very little butter and lots of eggs. Because you whisk the eggs for so long, they act as the raising agent and make the sponge super light, while instead of mountains of whipped cream between the layers, the honey-sweetened yogurt provides a creamy backdrop on which to load the berries.

Preheat the oven to 180°C/350°F/Gas 4. Line the bases of two 20cm/8in round sandwich tins with baking paper and grease the sides with a little low-calorie cooking oil spray.

Put the sugar and eggs in a large, heatproof bowl set over a saucepan of simmering water, then turn the heat down to low and whisk for 15–20 minutes, using an electric mixer, until really light and fluffy and doubled in size. You should be able to drip a W shape from the whisks, which should remain on the surface for 8 seconds.

Put the butter in a small saucepan over a low heat and when foaming, slowly whisk it into the egg mixture a drop at a time, whisking continuously. Gently fold in the flour, taking care not to overmix. Divide the mixture between the prepared tins and bake for 25 minutes, or until a skewer inserted in the centre comes out clean.

Turn the cakes out onto a wire rack to cool. Once cooled, use a serrated knife to cut each cake in half horizontally, giving you 4 discs. Spread one side of

Makes a 20cm/8in cake (12 servings)

low-calorie cooking oil spray, for greasing
50g/1¾oz/scant ¼ cup golden caster sugar
6 eggs
50g/1¾oz butter
250g/9oz/2 cups plain flour
2 tbsp low-sugar strawberry jam
430g/15¼oz/1¾ cups thick fat-free natural
    Greek yogurt
1 tbsp clear honey
600g/1lb 5oz/5 cups mixed summer berries

each cake disc with the jam. Mix together the yogurt and honey. Divide the yogurt among the 4 discs, spreading it out over the jam. Layer the cakes on top of each other, then load the top tier with fresh summer berries.

Lemon Tofu Cheesecake

PER SERVING:
    FAT 5.9G (OF WHICH SATURATES 2.4G)
    CALORIES 201KCAL
PREPARATION TIME: 30 MINUTES, PLUS
    1 HOUR CHILLING
COOKING TIME: 55 MINUTES

Replacing some of the cheese with super low-fat tofu creates a perfect low-fat cheesecake. Silken tofu has a similar texture to cream cheese and the strong flavour of lemon in the recipe means you will never know the difference.

Spray a 23cm/9in deep loose-based or springform cake tin with a little low-calorie cooking oil spray. Blend the biscuits to a fine crumb in a food processor. Put the butter and agave syrup in a small saucepan over a low heat until the butter has melted, then pour into the crumbs and blend again. Press the biscuit crumbs into the base of the prepared tin. Chill in the fridge for 1 hour until set.

Preheat the oven to 160°C/315°F/Gas 2½.

To make the cake, put the cream cheese in a food processor and blend until creamy, then add the agave syrup and butter and blend again. Add the tofu and blend once more, then add the eggs one at a time through the funnel and blend well between each addition. Finally add the milk, lemon juice, zest and cornflour. Blend everything together and then pour over the chilled biscuit base. Bake for 45 minutes, or until just set (you should still have a very slight wobble in the centre), then turn the oven off and open the door. Leave the cheese cake to cool in the oven until the oven is cold, then cover with a clean tea towel, making sure it does not touch the cake, and transfer to the fridge to chill.

Warm the raspberries in a small saucepan with the sugar and 1 tablespoon water so they start to release their juices, then leave to cool. Serve slices of the cheesecake with the cooled raspberries.

Makes a 23cm/9in cake (12 servings)

FOR THE BISCUIT BASE:
low-calorie cooking oil spray, for greasing
150g/5½oz low-fat digestive biscuits
35g/1¼oz butter
2 tbsp agave syrup

FOR THE LEMON TOFU FILLING:
200g/7oz light cream cheese
3 tbsp agave syrup
30g/1oz butter, softened
250g/9oz silken tofu, drained
2 eggs
3½ tbsp skimmed milk
grated zest and juice of 2 lemons
2 tbsp cornflour

TO SERVE:
400g/14oz/3¼ cups raspberries
1 tbsp caster sugar

 3 days 3 months

Carrot & Courgette Cake

PER SERVING:
FAT 5.5G (OF WHICH SATURATES 1G)
CALORIES 189KCAL
PREPARATION TIME: 15 MINUTES
COOKING TIME: 30 MINUTES

Everybody loves carrot cake because it is super moist and the natural sweetness of the carrots is highlighted by the spices. The addition of courgettes to this recipe means you can lower the fat content even further, as courgettes add extra moisture but without losing the carrot flavour. To my gorgeous niece Orlaith, this is known as my Peter Rabbit's Cake and it is a great recipe for kids, especially those who are a bit reluctant to eat their veggies, as it counts towards their five a day without them even noticing.

Preheat the oven to 180°C/350°F/Gas 4 and line a 20cm/8in square cake tin with baking paper.

Put the brown sugar, eggs and oil in a large bowl and whisk together for 3 minutes, using an electric mixer, to amalgamate and incorporate as much air as possible. Gently fold in the flour, bicarbonate of soda and spices and mix well, then stir in the grated carrots and courgettes.

Spoon the cake mixture into the prepared cake tin and bake in the centre of the oven for 25–30 minutes, or until a skewer inserted in the centre comes out clean.

Remove the cake from the oven, cover it with a tea towel and leave to cool in the tin for 10 minutes, then transfer to a wire rack, cover once again with the tea towel and leave to cool completely.

Mix together the cream cheese and sugar. Spread the topping over the cake and sprinkle with the chopped walnuts, then cut into 12 pieces to serve.

Makes a 20cm/8in square cake (12 servings)

FOR THE CARROT & COURGETTE CAKE:
150g/5½oz/heaped ¾ cup dark soft brown sugar
2 eggs
3 tbsp sunflower oil
200g/7oz/scant 1⅔ cups plain flour
1 tsp bicarbonate of soda
1 heaped tsp mixed spice
½ tsp ground ginger
2 tsp ground cinnamon
150g/5½oz carrots, peeled and grated
75g/2½oz courgettes, grated

FOR THE CREAM CHEESE TOPPING:
200g/7oz light cream cheese
2 tbsp caster sugar
4 walnuts, chopped

 3 days 3 months without icing

Devilishly Good Chocolate Mayonnaise Cake

PER SERVING:
    FAT 3.9G (OF WHICH SATURATES 2G)
    CALORIES 248KCAL
PREPARATION TIME: 25 MINUTES
COOKING TIME: 30 MINUTES

This recipe originally came from my mum. She recorded a similar recipe from a children's TV programme my sister was watching many years ago when we still recorded on VHS. My sister clearly remembers playing the video in the sitting room at a later date and running back and forth to the kitchen with the next instruction, only to then have to rewind it and play it back again. It does beg the question why did they not just watch it, write it down, then cook it. Thank goodness for internet print-outs now! I've adapted the recipe but the principle remains the same and uses mayonnaise in the ingredients. If you think about it, mayonnaise is simply egg yolks, oil and a dash of vinegar whisked together, and you always add eggs and a fat to a cake – either butter or oil. The only difference is that if you add mayonnaise, these two ingredients are already whisked together – with the added bonus that the vinegar reacts with baking powder to help the cake rise.

Preheat the oven to 180°C/350°F/Gas 4. Line the bases of two 20cm/8in round sandwich tins with baking paper and grease the sides with a little low-calorie cooking oil spray.

Mix together the flour, baking powder, cocoa powder and caster sugar in a large bowl. Tip the mayonnaise into the bowl but do not mix anything at this stage – however tempting that may be. Measure out 200ml/7fl oz/scant 1 cup boiling water, pour the water into the flour bowl and mix everything together thoroughly. Carefully pour the mixture into the prepared cake tins. Bake for 15–25 minutes, or until a skewer inserted in the centre comes out clean. Transfer to a wire rack to cool completely.

Makes a 20cm/8in cake (12 servings)

FOR THE CHOCOLATE CAKE:
low-calorie cooking oil spray, for greasing
300g/10½oz/heaped 2⅓ cups self-raising flour
1½ tsp baking powder
4 tbsp cocoa powder, sifted
175g/6oz/¾ cup caster sugar
200g/7oz/heaped ¾ cup light mayonnaise
a few pink rose petals, to decorate

FOR THE CHOCOLATE ICING:
35g/1¼oz butter
4 tbsp light evaporated milk
4 tbsp cocoa powder, sifted
175g/6oz/heaped 1⅓ cups icing sugar, sifted

 2 days   3 months

When the cake is cool, make the icing. Put the butter and evaporated milk in a small saucepan over a low heat until the butter has melted. Put the cocoa powder and icing sugar into the saucepan and mix everything together well. Remove from the heat and cover the surface of the icing with cling film, then leave to cool for 10 minutes until it is not quite so runny. (The cling film on the surface stops it from forming a 'skin'.)

Pour the cooled icing on top of the cake. Use a spatula to spread the icing towards the edges of the cake and allow it to run down the sides. Smooth the icing over the whole cake and either leave it with a smooth finish or add strokes of texture. Scatter the rose petals over the top to finish.

Chocolate Cloud Cake

PER SERVING:
   FAT 5.6G (OF WHICH SATURATES 2.5G)
   CALORIES 117KCAL
PREPARATION TIME: 10 MINUTES, PLUS
   20 MINUTES WHISKING AND CHILLING
   OVERNIGHT
COOKING TIME: 25 MINUTES

This cake is super rich so you can get your chocolate fix without over-eating. This is the dessert I often choose when I have friends for dinner who are gluten-intolerant. Everybody can enjoy the same dessert and no-one has to miss out – plus it's any chocoholic's dream.

Preheat the oven to 180°C/350°F/Gas 4. Spray a 23cm/9in, round, springform cake tin with low-calorie cooking oil spray and line the base with baking paper.

Bring 80ml/2½fl oz/⅓ cup water to the boil in a small saucepan. Add the cocoa powder and instant coffee and stir until smooth. Add the chocolate and vanilla extract and stir again until smooth.

Put the eggs, egg whites and caster sugar in a heatproof bowl and rest it over a pan of gently simmering water. Whisk for about 5 minutes, using an electric mixer, until thick and doubled in size. Remove from the heat and continue whisking for 15 minutes until it trails off the whisk in ribbons. You should be able to drip a W shape from the whisks, which should remain on the surface for 8 seconds.

Fold one-third of the egg mixture into the chocolate, then fold in the remainder. Spoon the mixture into the prepared tin and bake for 25 minutes, or until almost set with just a slight wobble in the centre.

Transfer the cake to a wire rack and leave to cool in the tin to room temperature, then chill for 8 hours or overnight.

Makes a 23cm/9in cake (12 servings)

low-calorie cooking oil spray, for greasing
30g/1oz/⅓ cup cocoa powder, sifted,
   plus 1 tsp for dusting
2 tsp instant coffee
125g/4½oz dark chocolate, 70% cocoa solids,
   finely chopped
½ tsp vanilla extract
3 eggs
3 egg whites
50g/1¾oz/scant ¼ cup caster sugar
1 tsp icing sugar, sifted, for dusting

 3 days ❄ 3 months without topping

Mix the icing sugar with the remaining cocoa powder, then sprinkle it over the cake to serve.

Earl Grey Tea Cake with Lemon & Passion Fruit

PER SERVING:
FAT 4.2G (OF WHICH SATURATES 0.4G)
CALORIES 213KCAL
PREPARATION TIME: 20 MINUTES
COOKING TIME: 30 MINUTES

Earl Grey tea is full of the heady aroma of bergamot. Its distinct taste and smell comes from the oil extracted from the zest of the bergamot orange, so it has a citrusy note that is perfect in this delicious cake with its lemony icing.

Preheat the oven to 180°C/350°F/Gas 4. Line the base of a 23cm/9in round loose-based cake tin with baking paper and spray the sides with a little low-calorie cooking oil spray.

Grind the tea leaves in a pestle and mortar until you have a fine powder. Sieve the tea, flour and baking powder into a bowl. Beat together the oil, caster sugar, eggs and pear purée, using an electric mixer, in a separate bowl. Pour this into the flour mixture and mix well.

Spoon the mixture into the prepared cake tin and bake for 30 minutes, or until a skewer inserted in the centre comes out clean. Transfer to a wire rack to cool completely.

Meanwhile, put the icing sugar in a bowl and gradually mix in enough of the lemon juice, a drop at a time, to make a thick paste that will dribble slowly down the sides of the cake. Drizzle the cake with the icing, then scatter with the passion fruit seeds to serve.

Makes a 23cm/9in cake (12 servings)

FOR THE EARL GREY TEA CAKE:
low-calorie cooking oil spray, for greasing
1½ tbsp loose-leaf Earl Grey tea (or you can simply empty 3 teabags)
250g/9oz/2 cups self-raising flour
2 tsp baking powder
3 tbsp sunflower oil
150g/5½oz/⅔ cup caster sugar
2 eggs
150g/5½oz tinned pears in natural juice, drained and puréed

FOR THE ICING:
150g/5½oz/1¼ cups icing sugar, sifted
1–2 tbsp lemon juice
1 passion fruit, halved and seeds scraped out

 3 days

Index

Acknowledgements

I just want to thank a few people for helping me get to this point – you baking from this book. My sister Joss, who helped out no end when it came to doing the admin things for me – without her I would have never made the deadline. Also Grace, who gave me the opportunity in the first place – it takes a leap of faith when taking on a new writer. Wendy, Grace and Jon for being so patient when I lost everything on my computer after it decided to crash. And finally Mum and Dad, who let me trash their kitchen as a child when I decided baking was the best form of entertainment – THANK YOU.

NOURISH

EAT WELL, LIVE WELL

We hope you've enjoyed this Nourish book. Here at Nourish we're all about wellbeing through food and drink – irresistible dishes with a serious good-for-you factor. If you want to eat and drink delicious things that set you up for the day, suit any special diets, keep you healthy and make the most of what you can afford, we've got some great ideas to share with you. Come over to our blog for wholesome recipes and fresh inspiration – nourishbooks.com.